Minnesota Housing Court Benchbook

Landlord Tenant Housing Court Law[1]

By Referee Mark Labine
Housing Court Referee – Hennepin County District Court

[1] **Updated November , 2011.**

Introduction

This Benchbook is a guide to help Judges work through Housing Court cases they have come before them.[2] The book consists of a checklist for the seven most common types of Housing Court cases. There is also a summary that discusses further legal issues Housing Court cases will present to Judges.

What's Unique about Landlord Tenant Law?

* Summary Proceeding – cases filed are required to be heard within 7-14 days of filing (Minn. Stat. 504B.331).

* Only civil case type where a party can seek an expungement (Minn. Stat. 484.014).

* Allow service by "Mail and Nail" – mailing and posting (Minn. Stat. 504B.331).

* Lay Advocates – Rule 603 of Housing Court Rules (Hennepin and Ramsey County) allows a lay advocate (not an attorney) to appear with a party at hearing if the party is an individual and is also present at the hearing.

* Agents – In Housing Court, agents are allowed to represent litigants in court with a Power of Authority. This is authorized by Minn. Stat. 481.02 and the Housing Court Rules for Hennepin and Ramsey Counties.

---

[2] A special thanks to Sophia Boschulte, my clerk, who spent numerous hours editing and reviewing this Benchbook.

Table of Contents

1. Eviction Case Checklist

Eviction Case Checklist

An eviction action is a summary proceeding, created by statute, to allow the landlord or person entitled to possession of property to evict the tenant or possessor of the property. The landlord commences an eviction case by preparing a written complaint and filing it with the court administrator, who prepares a summons. The defendant must be served at least seven days before the initial hearing, either by personal or substitute service, or by posting. Eviction actions are governed Minn. Stat. 504B et sec.

Housing Court Rule 603 applies to Housing Court cases heard in Hennepin County and Ramsey County. Minnesota Statute 481.02 applies to all the other Counties in Minnesota. In Hennepin County, this rule and statute allow a non-attorney agent to represent the owner, individual, Partnership, LLC or corporation if a power of authority is attached to the complaint at the time of filing. In other counties, however, including Ramsey, Corporations and LLC's are excepted from this practice and are required to be represented by Attorneys.

1. ☐ On Record, state parties present and address of property in question. Place names of party present in appearances section of Order form.

Agents may represent either party in Housing Court but a Power of Authority form must be filed first if the party is NOT an individual. If the party is an individual, you need a written Power of Authority unless the individual party is also present with the agent. (Rule 603 requires the Power of Authority to be filed with the complaint at the time of filing). You may receive a motion to dismiss because Landlord did not file the POA at the time of filing. Rule 6.02 of the Rules of Civil Procedure does allow the Court to extend the time requirement for "cause shown" so you do have discretion here.

Reason to state address is that on occasion Landlords list wrong address in complaint. Sheriff will only execute Writ on address as stated in complaint or order so if address wrong, Landlord will have to start over unless your order makes the correction. If address wrong and Tenant fails to show, you may have to require Landlord to start over since there will be a question about whether Tenant had proper notice.

2. ☐ Make sure Tenant has been properly served.

*Because Housing Court is a summary proceeding, Landlords may have a Housing Court case served either personally by a third party or by mail and posting. There must be at least **7 days** notice **unless case is an expedited case under in which case only 5 days notice required**[3]. If service by mail and posting, they have to file <u>four</u> affidavits in order for this to*

---

[3] Minn. Stat. 504B.321.

be done properly.   It is common for Tenants to raise service defenses in eviction actions. Minn. Stat. 504B.331 controls here.

*If Landlord has also brought a conciliation court action (Combo case) then service in conciliation court case must be **10 days** (13 days if by mail).*

3. ☐ Read complaint and ask Landlord if complaint true.

*Sometimes things have changed since the complaint was filed. Sometimes a partial payment has been made since the complaint was filed.   If a partial payment has been made on rent **in arrears**, demand copy of lease to see whether Landlord has waived the right to evict pursuant to Minn. Stat. 504B.291 subd 1(c). If lease has the language required by Minn. Stat. 504B.291, then you can proceed. If not, you may have to dismiss unless parties are willing to make an agreement.*

Most eviction actions are for non payment of rent. Most of these can be resolved quickly. Actions for breach of lease more complicated and usually have to be tried unless parties reach agreement.

4. ☐ If non payment of rent case, ask Tenant if agrees on what rent is owed. Find out what Tenant wants to do. Tenant has absolute right under Minn. Stat. 504B.291 subd. 1 to redeem by paying rent due plus costs and attorneys fees of $5.00.

*Most of time, there is no dispute on what rent is due. Often, Tenant will ask for some time to redeem and under the statute you can give them 7 days to do so. Also, Tenant will agree that some rent is due but not the amount alleged in complaint. In these situations, the Court has the option to place parties under oath and do a mini hearing on this issue to make a finding on the rent issue right away. Often there will be an undisputed amount of rent owed and perhaps an amount that is in dispute. Generally, if a trial is necessary, the court has the discretion to require the undisputed amount of rent owed plus rent that accrues pending the hearing placed into escrow pending the trial (in cash or certified funds only). The trial will then determine what amount of the disputed rent is in fact owed. **The order setting the hearing states that if Tenant does not deposit the money ordered into escrow that the hearing shall be cancelled and a Writ issued.** If Tenant cannot pay the undisputed amount of rent owed there is no reason to have a hearing on the disputed amount. Sometimes, the real problem is that Tenant simply does not have the money to pay the rent owed, and the deposit requirement will resolve the issue.   Often, when Tenants understand that this will happen, they are more willing to simply settle the case and work out either a payment agreement or they will agree to move out at some agreed date.*

The other option is to only require Tenant to pay the rent accruing pending the hearing which would generally be the current months rent.

Remember, there is NO RETALIATION DEFENSE TO A NON PAYMENT OF RENT CASE brought under Minn. Stat. 504B.291.[4]

5. ☐ In breach of lease cases, inquire about the nature of the dispute and try to narrow issue, if possible.

Often, the Tenant is willing to move out in breach of lease cases but simply wants more time. A little gentle persuasion by the Judge might help the parties to reach an agreement. (In Hennepin County, if necessary, the Judge can have the parties go back to Housing Court and use the Mediator assigned for that morning, if one is available).

If the issue is breach of lease, and you have to schedule a trial, you do not have to require Tenant to deposit rent owed or accruing pending the hearing if the allegation is for a "material breach of lease". (Minn. Stat. 504B.285 subd. 5). Whether a breach is "material" or not is your call.

6. ☐ If Tenant is raising defenses, review or discuss over them to determine whether they require an immediate dismissal.

Defenses where immediate dismissal may be appropriate:

- o *Improper service where affidavits of service not properly filed.*
- o *Landlord did not provide street address to Tenant as required by Minn. Stat. 504B.181 where not in dispute (P.O. Box not sufficient).*
- o *Partial payment of rent received for rent in arrears since action began or before but no written waiver as required by 504B.291.*
- o *Failure to attached POA to complaint as required by Rule 603 unless you allow more time under Rule 6.02 (Hennepin and Ramsey Counties only).*
- o *Landlord is a business entity using an assumed name and admits has not registered with state or filed an assumed name (other option is to continue case until this done and then fine them as allowed under Minn. Stat. 333.*

Defenses where you will probably have to schedule a hearing to make findings:

- o *Improper service where affidavits filed but Tenant alleges are untrue (denies being served).*
- o *Landlord is a business entity using an assumed name but it is alleged has not registered with state or filed an assumed name but Landlord disputes.*
- o *Landlord did not provide street address to Tenant as required by Minn. Stat. 504B.181 where in dispute (P.O. Box not sufficient).*
- o *Tenant alleges Landlord did not give copy of lease to him/her (This is NOT defense to non payment of rent case however) Minn. Stat. 504B.115 subd. 2.*

---

[4] See Minn. Stat. 504B.285 (breach of lease case) and Minn. Stat. 504B. 291 (non payment of rent case).

- o *Improper party listed as plaintiff.*
- o *Improper notice to vacate.*
- o *Fritz defense.*
- o *Eviction is a retaliation for Tenant asserting their rights only if eviction is for something other than non payment of rent. There is no retaliation defense for non payment of rent.*

Defenses where Judges and Referees have ruled both ways:

- o *Improper party listed as plaintiff.*
- o *Housing Authority has not been served with copy of complaint in Section 8 case.*[5]

7. ☐ If Tenant alleges FRITZ defense, then you need to have Tenant deposit rent owed into Court and schedule hearing.

A Fritz defense is allowed pursuant to the case: <u>Fritz v. Warthen,</u> 298 Minn. 54, 213 N.W.2d 339 (Minn. 1973)[6]. *If Tenant asserts and Court determines that an issue regarding a*

---

[5] This is issue of "Condition Precedent". In all Section 8 cases there are three parties involved: Landlord, Tenant, and the Housing Authority. The Housing Authority will rarely be a party to the action. However, in all Section 8 cases the Landlord has a contract with the Housing Authority which states that a Tenancy Addendum (Part C) must be attached to the lease which requires Landlord to serve a copy of the Eviction action on the Housing Authority at the same time the eviction action is served on Tenant. The Tenant has a right to enforce this provision. If the Housing Authority is not served, Landlord is in violation of the lease requirement that the Housing Authority be served. The question is then raised should the Court dismiss based on this breach, proceed with action and address this breach at trial, or should the Court require service or Joinder as allowed by Rule 19 of the Rules of Civil Procedure? Often the Tenant will admit they are in breach of the lease also by owing rent so you have a situation where both parties are in breach. What is the right thing to do?

A rule in the law of contracts is that a party cannot raise to its advantage a breach of contract against another party when it has first breached the contract itself. <u>MTS vs. Taiga</u> 365 N.W.2d 321 (Minn. App. 1985) <u>Cheezem Development Corp. v. Intracoastal Sales and Service, Inc.</u>, 336 So.2d. 1210, 1212 (Fla.Ct.App.1976); <u>Yonan v. Oak Park Federal Savings and Loan Association</u>, 326 N.E.2d 773, 781 (Ill.App.1975); <u>Robinhorne Construction Corp. v. Snyder, 251 N.E.2d 641</u>, 645-46 (Ill.App.1969), aff'd, 265 N.E.2d 670 (Ill.1970). Cf. <u>Verran v. Blacklock</u>, 60 Mich.App. 763, 231 N.W.2d 544, 547 (1975); <u>Odysseys Unlimited, Inc. v. Astral Travel Service</u>, 77 Misc.2d 502, 354 N.Y.S.2d 88, 91 (Sup.Ct.1974). **While this rule should not apply in every case to prevent the initial breaching party from seeking a remedy for another party's subsequent breach**, in the Taiga case the rule was applied because in that case Plaintiff's initial breach was a cause of the alleged breach by defendant. Usually in these Landlord Tenant relationships, the failure by the Landlord to notify HUD in violation of the lease is not a "first breach" and usually has no relationship to the breach of tenant which is either breach of lease or non payment of rent.

Clearly where Landlord must satisfy a "condition precedent" as required by HUD regulations the remedy would be to dismiss the case. See <u>Hoglund-Hall v. Kleinschmidt</u> 381 N.W. 889 (Minn. App. 1986) (case dismissed because Landlord failed to give Tenant written notice of the breach prior to commencing eviction action) and also <u>Majors v. Green Meadows Apartments</u>, 546 F.Supp. 895, 903 (S.D.Ga.1981) (where lease provision contradicts FmHA regulations, the regulations control).

breach of covenant of habitability exists, the Court should order all rent due and accruing rent be deposited into Court pending the hearing.

8. ☐ If Combo Case, you need to address money issue as well as the Housing Court issue of possession (Hennepin County only).

Generally, Housing Court cases ONLY deal with the issue of possession and claims for unpaid rent are dealt with in Conciliation Court. In COMBO cases, however, Landlords do have the right to ask you address the issue of back rent owed if they bring a conciliation court action and have properly served Tenants. These agreements may be mediated but ALL parties, mediator and Judge MUST sign the mediation agreement in Combo cases. Also, note that in conciliation court cases there is a 72 hour right to rescind the mediation agreement. This is not so in Housing and make sure the mediation agreement does not allow parties to rescind the Housing Court agreement within 72 hours.

9. ☐ Encourage Settlement. If possible, get parties to talk to a Mediator if available. (In Hennepin County a Mediator is usually available in Housing Court on all First Appearance Calendar days). If parties can settle without Mediator, we suggest they use the Housing Court Settlement forms (a copy is included in the Benchbook under section 8). Settlements should be in writing.

10. ☐ If Case cannot be resolved at First Appearance, then schedule trial on issues raised.

Discuss how trial will be conducted and determine whether parties need an order disclosing witnesses and exhibits prior the trial. Remind parties to bring at least 3 copies of all exhibits to the trial. Parties do have the right to a Jury trial in Eviction cases. **Trial must be set within 6 business days unless parties otherwise agree.**

11. ☐ Order form to schedule trial provided in the Benchbook.

> *a – Address discovery issues. (Because of summary nature of Housing, generally only discovery is to require parties to give notice of witnesses and copies of exhibits on some date prior to hearing.)*

---

6 The Fritz case holds that once the trial court has determined that a fact question exists as to the breach of the covenants of habitability, that court will order the tenant to pay the rent to be withheld from the landlord into court and that until final resolution on the merits, any future rent withheld shall also be paid into court.

b – Order rent deposited if applicable. Deposit usually must be done by next day between hours of 8:00 a.m. and 4:00 p.m. at the Housing Court Counter. (In Hennepin County the counter is closed on Wednesday afternoons from 1:30 p.m. until closing.

c – Order Interpreter if one needed.

d – Send all parties back to Housing Court with the file for trial date (Hennepin County only).

e – Make sure you check all boxes in order form that you want to apply.

12. ☐ Conduct trial on issues raised.

Try to narrow the issues as much as possible before the trial begins. If Jury Trial, try to agree on what issue or question will be presented to the Jury before the trial begins rather than waiting until the end.

13. ☐ Prepare Findings and Order ASAP.

*Housing Court cases are summary proceedings and it is important to get orders out as soon as possible. Orders should give specific findings and remember **not to order expungement** unless nothing further is to happen on case. The parties can move to expunge the file after everything in your order has been completed.*

NOTE: If order allows a Writ, remember you can stay issuance of Writ up to 7 days under Minn. Stat. 504B.345 subd. 1 (d). Stays are also allowed during Appeals (See Section 9 Summary regarding Appeals).

14. ☐ Costs.

*In Hennepin County the Clerks in Housing Court are instructed to **not** award costs unless the order allows it. Other Districts may have different rules. Costs are generally not allowed unless a judgment is entered. If there is a settlement or an order allowing redemption, usually no judgment is entered unless order clearly states as such.*

If you do not check the allowable costs box or otherwise allow costs to the prevailing party, they will not get the costs if and when a judgment is entered. All prevailing parties in Housing Court cases generally are allowed $205.50 in costs as set out in Minn. Stat. 549.02.

Other Notes [7]

---

[7] Information in "Notes" obtained from "Residential Unlawful Detainer and Eviction Defense", Ninth Edition (2004) by Lawrence R. McDonough.

"Unlawful Detainer is a civil proceeding, and the only issue for determination is whether the facts alleged in the complaint are true." This often quoted statement by the Minnesota Court of Appeals has lulled many a landlord and tenant, as well as their counsel, into thinking that all eviction cases are simple matters of whether the tenant paid the rent, breached the lease, or failed to vacate after expiration of a lease or getting proper notice from the landlord. To the contrary, the law of evictions is a complex mixture of state statutes governing evictions and general landlord-tenant relations, the common law of property and contracts, and federal law governing fair housing and public and subsidized housing programs.

In most courts, the initial hearing serves as an arraignment. If the defendant does not appear, the court will enter a judgment for the plaintiff and issue a writ of recovery, formerly a writ of restitution. If the defendant appears to contest the action, the court generally will schedule a trial for another day. If the defendant appears and does not contest the action, the court will find for the plaintiff, but might stay issuance of the writ of recovery for up to seven days. The court may continue the trial for up to six days without consent of the parties; or longer with consent, or in certain circumstances, up to three months for a material witness if a bond is paid. The Housing Court rules provide for discovery and the Court may allow discovery as long as it can be completed within the 6 days.

The court may require the defendant to post rent or other security as a precondition to a trial or to raising a defense, including: continuance beyond six days for lack of a material witness.

It is not uncommon for the plaintiff to raise additional issues not pleaded in the complaint at the initial hearing or trial. Rule 15 of the Rules of Civil Procedure control here. The primary concern is prejudice to the Tenant and if the Court does decide to amend the complaint, the Court should ensure that there is sufficient time for Tenant to prepare a defense to the amended complaint.

At trial, the plaintiff has the burden of proof by preponderance of the evidence, and the defendant may raise numerous statutory and common law defenses. The parties are entitled to a full trial, and may demand a trial by jury. The summary nature of the action does not relieve the court of the obligation to find facts specially and state separately its conclusions of law. Failure to include findings usually requires reversal, unless the decision necessarily decides all disputed facts, or the undecided issues are immaterial.

If the tenant prevails, the landlord may not evict the tenant at this time. If the landlord prevails, the court may immediately issue a writ of recovery or stay issuance of the writ for up to seven days. The landlord then must arrange for the sheriff to deliver the writ, which is a 24-hour eviction notice. If the tenant does not move, the landlord must schedule an eviction of the tenant with the sheriff or police. The landlord must store the tenant's property, either on site or with a storage company, for up to 28 days[8] (2010 law effective August 1, 2010). Either party may appeal from entry of judgment within ten days of entry of judgment.

An eviction judgment does not prevent the tenant from raising in another action an issue that could have been raised in the eviction action but was not raised, or was raised but later withdrawn; an issue raised in the eviction action, which the court declined to rule on, or issues of title. The primary issue in Housing Court cases is possession of the leased property. A determination of possession does not prevent either party from bringing a money claim for back rent owed, damages, rent abatement, or issues regarding the security deposit.

MNCIS Note: The Eviction order form shown below is available in MINCIS under "forms" which you select after you open up the case assigned to you.

---

[8] Law up to August 1, 2010 is 60 days. This will be reduced to 28 days effective August 1, 2010. Minn. Stat. 504B.271.

State of Minnesota	District Court
Hennepin	Judicial District: Court File Number: Case Type:　　　　　Housing

Plaintiff

of

Eviction Action – Findings

**Fact, Conclusions of Law,
Order and Judgment
(Minn. Stat. § 504B.285, 504B.345)**

vs.

Defendant

This case was heard by the undersigned on _____.

Date

PLAINTIFF: Represented by: ☐ counsel   ☐
agent
☐ Appeared in person.
☐ Did not appear and is in default.
_____
                                                    _____
                                                              Name

DEFENDANT: Represented by: ☐ advocate   ☐
counsel
☐ Appeared in person.
☐ Did not appear and is in default.
_____
                                                    _____
                                                              Name

Defendant has ☐ admitted ☐ denied   the allegations in the Eviction Action complaint.

Findings Of Fact And Conclusions Of Law

1.　☐　Plaintiff has failed to prove the allegations in the complaint.

2.　☐　COMPLAINT:
　　　　Plaintiff proved the following allegations by a preponderance of the evidence.
　　　　☐　a.　Compliance with Minn. Stat. § 504B.181.
　　　　☐　b.　Nonpayment of rent

☐ c. Defendant has failed and refuses to pay rent for the month(s) of
_____ _____ in the amount of $_____
_____ per month payable on the _____ day of each month for a
total due of $ _____.

☐ d. Notice to vacate was properly given and Defendant has failed to vacate
said property.

☐ e. Defendant has broken the terms of the rental agreement and Defendant
has failed to vacate the
property_____.

☐ f. Defendant mortgagor(s) failed to timely redeem after mortgage foreclosure
sale.

☐ g. Other: _____.

3. ☐ DEFENSES:
Defendant(s) proved the following defenses by a preponderance of the evidence.

☐ a. Improper service by _____.

☐ b. Violation of the covenants of habitability by _____
_____
_____.

☐ c. Improper notice because _____.

☐ d. Waiver of _____ by _____.

☐ e. Other: _____

4. ☐ SETTLEMENT: **No judgment to be entered at this time**
The parties have reached a settlement, which is approved and incorporated in this

Decision and Order.

☐ Settled through Mediation (See attached settlement agreement)
☐ Settled by the Litigants (See attached settlement agreement)
☐ Settlement terms are as follows: _____
_____
_____

Order

1. ☐ The settlement is hereby approved as agreed upon.

2. ☐ JUDGMENT:
The Court Administrator shall enter judgment for:

☐ a. **Plaintiff** for recovery of the premises. The Writ of Recovery of Premises
and Order to Vacate shall be:

☐ i. issued immediately upon request and payment of fee.

☐ ii. stayed until _____
Date

☐ b. **Defendant** to remain in possession of the premises.

    ☐ c. **Allowable costs and disbursements** to the prevailing party.

3. ☐ DISMISSAL:
The case is dismissed   ☐ WITH   ☐ WITHOUT prejudice and the Court Administrator shall enter Judgment accordingly.

4. ☐ REDEMPTION:

Defendant may redeem the premise (for nonpayment of rent) by paying to the Plaintiff $_____ by _____. If not, a judgment and writ shall issue by default.

5. ☐ RENT ABATEMENT:
Defendant has had diminished use and enjoyment of the premises. Rent is abated for the months of _____ by a total of $_____ _____, and is abated by $_____ per month until the first month following completion of court ordered repairs.

6. ☐ RENT DISBURSEMENT:
The rent now on deposit with the Court shall be released as follows:
☐ $_____ to Plaintiff   ☐ $_____ to Defendant

7. ☐ HEARING:
This is scheduled for ☐ court trial ☐ jury trial ☐ motion hearing on issues of

_____

_____ _____ on _____, at _____
_____ (a.m./p.m.). Both parties shall come to A-1700 Government Center (OR_____) for courtroom assignment.

8. ☐ DISCOVERY:
The parties shall provide to each other by _____, _____,   the following: a list of witnesses, with phone numbers and addresses, and the subjects about which they will testify, and copies of exhibits (documents, photographs, etc.) to be introduced at trial, and _____

_____.

9. ☐ RENT INTO COURT:
Defendant shall pay into Court the rent of $_____ in   cash   or certified   funds   payable   to   the   Court   Administrator,   on   or   before _____(a.m./p.m.) on _____,___, and all future rent by the _____ day of each month until further Order of the Court, or the Court will issue a Writ of Recovery of Premises and Order to Vacate.

10. ☐ OTHER: _____.

☐ **Let Judgment Be Entered Accordingly**

By the Court:

_____   _____
Judge   Date

Judgment

I hereby certify that the above Order constitutes the entry of Judgment of the Court.

Dated: _____   Court Administrator
                                              By: _____
                                                       Deputy

2. Rent Escrow Case Checklist

Rent Escrow Case Checklist

Rent Escrow cases are governed by Minn. Stat. 504B.385.   If Landlord is in violation of a law, building code, or obligation as set forth in Minn. Stat. 504B et sec. in a residential building, a **residential tenant** may deposit the amount of rent due to the landlord with the court   administrator using the procedures described in 504B.385.

1. ☐ Verify names of parties and address of leased property.

Need to verify who owners or Management Company is. Sometimes there is confusion as to who Tenant is dealing with. Often there is an owner and a Manager and both may need to be served.

2. ☐ Make sure Landlord has been properly served.

3. ☐ Make sure all rent owed has been deposited.

Need to verify how much rent is owed which usually can be done by looking at lease.   Landlord will certainly help you determine this. If legitimate dispute, this can be addressed at the hearing. If all rent required to be deposited is not put into escrow, then case can be dismissed.

4. ☐ Try to get parties to agree on what repairs are needed or what else Landlord needs to
do to comply with the law. In other words, what is basis for Tenant's complaint.

If repairs are needed, it can greatly simplify the trial if the parties agree on what repairs need to be done. Even if Landlord did not get sufficient notice, it makes sense to address the repair issues now rather than have the parties maybe come back later. If there is something else the Landlord is not in compliance with (e.g. no rental license) try to list that in order.

The advantage of doing it this way is that the Landlord has incentive to come into compliance before the hearing and then you will not have to schedule another compliance hearing to ensure that Landlord makes the needed or required repairs or other actions to come into compliance. You can then focus the hearing on the issue of rent abatement and other money penalties only.

5. ☐ Schedule a hearing. (Note: <u>NO right to Jury trial for rent escrow cases</u>).

6. ☐ Conduct trial on issues raised in rent escrow affidavit and answer of Landlord.

If Landlord has made all required repairs or is now in compliance with the law, then it can greatly simplify the trial.   If there are still things that need to be done, you will have to determine those and then probably schedule another compliance hearing to ensure that Landlord complies with your order.

All rent escrow cases involve some breach of law, code, or other obligation of the Landlord. Try to determine what the breach is. If repairs needed, try to determine whether Landlord had 14 days to make repairs as statute requires.

7. ☐ Issue Findings and Order. If necessary, schedule a compliance hearing to ensure Landlord complies with order. You may allow rent to continue to be placed in escrow until all repairs done.

Possible remedies set out in Minn. Stat. 504B.385 subd. 9. Remember, you have a lot of discretion here. Rent abatement is most common remedy asked for. (See TRA checklist for more info on Rent Abatement).

Other Notes

The classic set of facts which would qualify Tenant to bring a rent escrow action is that the Housing Inspector has inspected the leased property and noted building code violations at the leased property which Landlord needs to fix.

The residential tenant may not deposit the rent or file the written notice of the code violation until the time granted by the Housing Inspector to make the repairs has expired without satisfactory repairs being made, unless the residential tenant alleges that the time granted is excessive.

If there are other repairs needed at the leased property for which Landlord is responsible to make, the residential tenant must give written notice to the landlord specifying the violation. The notice must be delivered personally or sent to the person or place where rent is normally paid. If the violation is not corrected within 14 days, the residential tenant may deposit the amount of rent due to the landlord with the court administrator along with an affidavit specifying the violation.

Issue of Notice and Rent Abatement. There is an issue about whether or not Tenant is required to give written notice of the violations prior to commencing a rent escrow case or as a condition for asking for rent abatement. Clearly, under Minn. Stat. 504B.385, 14 days written notice is required. It is fair and equitable to expect that Landlord be made aware of a repair problem before assessing a penalty against Landlord. This argument supports the conclusion that no rent abatement should be allowed until after Landlord received notice of the repair issue. However, there is an argument that once you have decided that Tenant is properly before the court, then the issue of rent abatement is determined by how long the Tenant had subpar housing and how long the Landlord knew or should have known about the repair problems. In an unpublished case titled <u>Richtor v.Czock</u>, 2002 WL 338181 (Minn. App.), The Court of Appeals held as follows:

> Under <u>Minn.Stat. § 504B.425(a), (e) (2000)</u>, if the court finds that a violation of clause (1) or (2) of <u>Minn.Stat. 504B.161, subd. 1</u>, has been proved, in its discretion,

> [t]he court may find the extent to which any uncorrected violations impair the residential tenants' use and enjoyment of the property contracted for and order the **rent abated** accordingly. If the court enters judgment under this paragraph, the parties shall be informed and the court shall determine the amount by which the **rent** is to be **abated.** (Emphasis added.) See also <u>Minn.Stat. § § 504B.395, subd. 1(1)</u> (procedure for bringing tenants' action), .001, subd. 14(2) (2000) (defining violation).

> Under this statute, the court has discretion to order **rent abatement;** it is not required to order **abatement.** Compare <u>Minn.Stat. § 645.44, subd. 15 (2000)</u> (stating " 'may' is permissive") with <u>Minn.Stat. § 645.44, subd. 16 (2000)</u> (stating " 'shall' is mandatory"). Appellants have not shown that the district court abused its discretion in **abating rent** only during the period that it was shown that the **landlord knew about the violations.**

The Czock decision appears to support the proposition that rent abatment is reasonable during any period that Landlord knew about the violations.

There are a series of tort cases that have held that a Landlord who violated covenants of habitability had a duty to warn the Tenant of the defective condition if the Landlord knew or should have known of the violations or danger. See **Oakland v. Stenlund** 420N.W.2d 248, Minn.App.,1988, which stated the duties of a Landlord to warn are as follows:

> [W]here a landlord has information which would lead a reasonably prudent owner exercising due care to suspect that danger exists on the leased premises at the time the tenant takes possession, and that the tenant exercising due care would not discover it for himself, then he must at least disclose such information to the tenant. * * *

> "To require one to use that care which an ordinarily prudent person would exercise under the same or similar circumstances can hardly be onerous,unreasonable or oppressive." (quoting the trial court memorandum) citing <u>Johnson v. O'Brien</u>, 258 Minn. 502, 5105 N.W.2d 244 (1960).

Conclusion: It is reasonable for a court to award rent abatement for loss of use or impaired value of the rental until for any period that Landlord know or should have known about a defective or impaired condition.

Deposit of Rent. The residential tenant need not deposit rent if none is due to the landlord at the time the residential tenant files the rent escrow action. All rent which becomes due to the landlord after that time but before the hearing under subdivision 6 must be deposited with the Court Administrator. As long as proceedings are pending under this section, the residential tenant must pay rent to the landlord or as directed by the court and may not withhold rent to remedy a violation.

Counterclaim for possession. The landlord may file a counterclaim for possession of the property in cases where the landlord alleges that the residential tenant did not deposit the full amount of rent with the court administrator.

Notice of hearing. A hearing must be held within ten to 14 days from the day a residential tenant deposits rent with the court administrator.

Judgment. Upon finding that a violation exists, the court may, in its discretion, do any or all of the following:

(1) order relief as provided in section 504B.425, including retroactive rent abatement;

(2) order that all or a portion of the rent in escrow be released for the purpose of remedying the violation;

(3) order that rent be deposited with the court as it becomes due to the landlord or abate future rent until the landlord remedies the violation; or

(4) impose fines as required in section 504B.391.

(5) When a proceeding under this section has been consolidated with a counterclaim for possession or an eviction action, and the landlord prevails, the residential tenant may redeem the tenancy as provided in section 504B.291.

(6) When a proceeding under this section has been consolidated with a counterclaim for possession or an eviction action on the grounds of nonpayment, the court may not require the residential tenant to pay the landlord's filing fee as a condition of retaining possession of the property when the residential tenant has deposited with the court the full amount of money found by the court to be owed to the landlord.

Release of rent after hearing. If the court finds, after a hearing on the matter has been held, that no violation exists in the building or that the residential tenant did not deposit the full amount of rent due with the court administrator, it shall order the immediate release of the rent to the landlord. If the court finds that a violation existed, but was remedied between the commencement of the action and the hearing, it may order rent abatement and must release the rent to the parties accordingly. Any rent found to be owed to the residential tenant must be released to the tenant.

State of Minnesota   **District Court**

Judicial District:
Court File Number:
Case Type: Housing

_____

Plaintiff

                                                         Rent Escrow Order

vs.

_____

Defendant
_____

This case was heard by the undersigned on _____.
                                                                    Date

PLAINTIFF: Represented by: ☐ counsel   ☐ agent
☐ Appeared in person.
☐ Did not appear and is in default.   _____
_____   Name

DEFENDANT: Represented by: ☐ advocate   ☐
counsel
☐ Appeared in person.
☐ Did not appear and is in default.   _____
_____   Name

      Based upon the verified petition, testimony, evidence, and arguments presented, and all of the files, records, and proceedings, the Court makes the following:

Findings Of Fact And Conclusions Of Law

1. ☐ Plaintiff leases residential premises from Defendant located at _____
_____.

2. ☐ Rent for the property is $_____ per month.

3. ☐ Plaintiff has deposited $_____ with the Clerk of Court.

4. ☐ The premises were found to be in violation of Minn. Stat. 504B.161 as noted in a written order by the local Department of Inspections dated _____. The date set for correction was _____.

5. ☐ The Plaintiff gave written notice of violations to the Defendant on or about - _____.

6. ☐ The date set by the Department of Inspections passed without completion of corrections; the date set was excessive because _____.

7. ☐ Fourteen days elapsed without completion of repairs required in Plaintiff's notice.

8. ☐ Violations do not exist at the property.

9. ☐ Violations exist at the property as follows: _____

_____.

Order

1. ☐ The rent in the amount of $_____ per month is abated by $_____ per month. The amount due to Defendant for months of _____ is $_____.

2. ☐ Plaintiff's claim for rent abatement is denied.

3. ☐ It is ordered that the rent now on deposit shall be released as follows:

$_____ to Plaintiff

$_____ to Defendant

$_____ to Defendant upon a showing that ordered repairs have been completed

4. ☐ Future monthly rent is abated by $_____ and the balance of $_____ shall be _____paid directly to Defendant, or _____paid to the Clerk of Court, in cash or certified funds, to be released to Defendant upon a showing that ordered repairs have been completed.

5. ☐ Rent abatement shall terminate for the first rental period following Defendant's completion of repairs.

6. ☐ Defendant is ordered to remedy violations on or before _____.

7.   ☐ Both parties shall appear at a compliance hearing set on _____ at _____ a.m. / p.m. at _____.

8.   ☐ The Clerk of Court shall either give to the parties or mail to the parties by first class mail a copy of this Order.

9.   ☐ Other:

_____

Let Judgment Be Entered Accordingly

By the Court:

_____   Dated:_____

Judge

3. Tenant Remedy Action Checklist

TRA Checklist

Tenant Remedy Actions (TRA's) fall under Minn. Stat. 504B.395 to 504B.471. These are actions brought by the Tenant or on behalf of the Tenant to ask the Court to address code violations or defects in residential rental units.

Comparison of Rent escrow cases to TRA's. Both Rent Escrow cases and TRA's require that notice be given to Landlord's prior to the commencement of the action to give Landlord's a reasonable opportunity to fix the problem.

	Rent Escrow	Tenant Remedy Action (TRA)
Filing Fee 2010	$70	$322
Rent Deposit	All rent owed	None unless ordered by Court as allowed under Minn. Stat. 504B.425
Proper Party	Person named in lease as Tenant	Tenant, All other tenants in building, City Attorney, Neighborhood Organizations

Per motion passed by the Civil Committee for the Hennepin County District Court on April 20, 2009, **Housing Court Rule 603 applies to Housing Court cases heard in Hennepin County District Court by Judges.** This rule allows a non-attorney agent to represent the owner, individual or corporation if a power of authority is attached to the complaint at the time of filing.

1. ☐ On Record, state the parties present and the address of property in question. Put names of parties present in order.

Often names are misspelled or even wrong parties named. This needs to be clarified. Make sure the rental property listed is in the proper County.

2. ☐ Make sure Plaintiff is a proper party as set out in Minn. Stat. 504B.395, subd. 1. Review lease if one exists.

Proper party is 1) residential tenant, 2) Housing-related neighborhood organization with written permission from residential tenant, 3) Housing-related neighborhood organization with unoccupied residential unit within its boundaries and 4) a state, County, or local department or authority charged with enforcement of Housing Codes.

3. ☐ Make sure Landlord has been properly served.

Service rules different for TRA as compared to Eviction action. See Minn. Stat. 504B.401. Generally personal service or can mail and post. Service must be not less than 5 or more than 10 days before hearing.

4. ☐ Read petition and ask Tenant if petition is true. Clarify code violation.

In most cases Plaintiff should have a Housing Inspection report to verify the problem.

5. ☐ Verify that Landlord had 14 days notice of the violation or that Landlord could not be located after diligent efforts.

Minn. Stat. 504B.395 subd. 4 states Landlord must be notified at least 14 days before the action commenced. The idea behind this law is to give Landlord a chance to repair the code violation.

6. ☐ Determine what needs to be done to get the code violations fixed. Conduct hearing if necessary. <u>No right to jury trial here!</u> (Minn. Stat. 504B.421).

Often, you can figure out the problem pretty quickly. Usually a Housing Inspection report exists. Housing Inspection reports are admissible evidence under Minn. Stat. 504B.385 subd 6 if they are certified.[9]

7. ☐ If necessary, schedule a compliance hearing to make sure your order is carried out. Determine whether Tenant's rent should be placed into escrow with the Court.

8. ☐ Prepare Findings and Order ASAP.

Housing Court cases are summary proceedings and it is important to get orders out as soon as possible. Orders should give specific findings.

9. ☐ Rent Abatement.

Under Minn.Stat. § 504B.425(a), (e) (2000), if the court finds that a violation of clause (1) or (2) of Minn.Stat. 504B.161, subd. 1, has been proved, in its discretion, [t]he court may find the extent to which any uncorrected violations impair the residential tenants' use and enjoyment of the property contracted for and order the rent abated accordingly. If the court enters judgment under this paragraph, the parties shall be informed and the court shall determine the amount by which the rent is to be abated. (Emphasis added.) See also Minn.Stat. §§ 504B.395, subd. 1(1) (procedure for bringing tenants' action), .001, subd. 14(2) (2000) (defining violation).

Under this statute, the court has discretion to order rent abatement; it is not required to order abatement. Compare Minn.Stat. § 645.44, subd. 15 (2000) (stating " 'may' is permissive") with Minn.Stat. § 645.44, subd. 16 (2000) (stating " 'shall' is mandatory"). Under both Minn.Stat. § 566.25 and Minn.Stat. § 566.34, subd. 10, the district court "may, in its discretion," order one or more of several possible remedies including rent abatement. Minn.Stat. §§ 566.25(d); 566.34, subd. 10(a)(1). The statutes' use of "may" combined with their non-exclusive lists of remedies show that no particular remedy is mandatory and that the district court has broad discretion to select the remedy appropriate to the facts of the case. <u>Scroggins v. Solchaga</u> 552 N.W. 2d 248, (Minn. App. 1996).

---

[9] 504B.385 Subd. 6. **"Hearing.** The hearing shall be conducted by a court without a jury. A certified copy of an inspection report meets the requirements of rule 803(8) of the Minnesota Rules of Evidence as an exception to the rule against hearsay, and meets the requirements of rules 901 and 902 of the Minnesota Rules of Evidence as to authentication."

If the Court were to award Plaintiff rent abatement, it must find that the uncorrected violations impairs the Tenant's use and enjoyment of the property.   If Landlord does not have a rental license (a violation of the law), the Court also "may" order rent abatement but is not required to.

10. ☐ Costs.

*The Clerks in Hennepin County Housing Court are instructed to **not** award costs unless the order allows.*

All prevailing parties in Housing Court cases generally are allowed $205.50 in costs as set out in Minn. Stat. 549.02.

Remember if an IFP was filed, no costs have yet been paid into court.   If Tenant prevails, you can order Landlord to pay the filing fee to the court as part of the remedy.

State of Minnesota

Judicial District:
Court File Number:
Case Type: Housing

_____

Plaintiff

**ORDER ON PETITION FOR
RELIEF UNDER TENANT
REMEDIES ACT
MINNESOTA STATUTE
504B.395**

vs.

_____

Defendant

This case was heard by the undersigned on _____.

Date

PLAINTIFF: Represented by: ☐ counsel   ☐ agent
☐ Appeared in person.
☐ Did not appear and is in default.
_____   _____
                                                                        Name

DEFENDANT: Represented by: ☐ advocate   ☐ counsel
☐ Appeared in person.
☐ Did not appear and is in default.
                                                             _____
                                                                        Name

　　　Based upon the verified petition, testimony, evidence, and arguments presented, and all of the files, records, and proceedings, the Court makes the following:

Findings Of Fact And Conclusions Of Law

　　　1.　☐　Plaintiff(s) is/are an interested party as defined under Minn. Stat. 504B.395.

　　　2.　☐　Plaintiff(s) is/are a legal authority charged with the enforcement of codes relating to the health, housing and building maintenance at the subject property.

　　　3.　☐　　　The　　property　　in　　issue　　is　　located　　at
_____.

　　　4.　☐ Plaintiff(s) is/are a tenant at the property.

5. ☐ The   name   and   address   of   the   defendant(s)   is/are

_____

_____.

6. ☐ Defendant(s) is/are the owner(s) and/or manager(s) of the property.

7. ☐ Notice to defendant(s): The City Inspector ordered the building owner(s) or manager(s) to repair the property by the following date: _____.

8. ☐ The owner(s) and manager(s) did complete the repairs on time.

9. ☐ The owner(s) and manager(s) did NOT complete the repairs on time.

10. ☐ Plaintiff pays rent in the amount of $_____ each month which is due on the _____ day of each month.

11. ☐ The repairs needed at the property are:

12. ☐ Actions of plaintiff(s):

    ☐ a. The problems with the housing are **not** the result of the deliberate or negligent act or omission of plaintiff(s) or anyone acting under plaintiff(s)' direction or control.

    ☐ b. The problems with the housing are the result of the deliberate or negligent act or omission plaintiff(s) or a person acting under plaintiff(s)' direction or control.

13. ☐ The parties have reached a settlement of this matter.

14. ☐ Other _____.

Based upon the above Findings of Fact and Conclusions of Law, the court makes the following:

ORDER

1. ☐ Plaintiff(s)' request for relief is denied.

2. ☐ Plaintiff(s)' request for relief is granted as follows (check all that apply):

    a. ☐ Defendant(s) shall take the following action to immediately fix the following   problems:

    _____

_____

_____The repairs shall be made on or before _____.

b. ☐ Plaintiff(s) shall fix the problem(s) and deduct the cost up to the amount of $_____ from the rent for each of the following months: _____.

c. ☐ On or before _____ plaintiff(s) shall deposit with the court administrator rent in the amount of $_____ to be held in escrow.

d. ☐ An administrator shall take over operation of the property to fix the problems. The name of the administrator is: _____.

e. ☐ On or before _____ defendant(s) shall pay to plaintiff(s) a rent refund or credit in the total amount of $_____ for the problems that existed during the month(s) of _____.

f. ☐ Defendant(s) shall give Plaintiff(s) a future rent credit each month in the amount of $_____ until the problems are fixed.

g. ☐ If defendant(s) violates this Order, defendant(s) shall be fined $_____.

h. ☐ On or before _____ defendant(s) shall pay to plaintiff(s) attorney's fees and costs in the amount of $_____.

i. ☐ On or before _____ defendant(s) shall pay to plaintiff(s) costs in the amount of $_____.

j. ☐ The terms of Settlement Agreement are approved and agreed upon and incorporated into this order

3. ☐ Other:_____

4. ☐ The defendant shall submit to the court and plaintiff(s) written proof from the City Inspector that the repairs described above have been completed.

5. ☐ This matter is scheduled for a hearing on _____ at _____ _____.m. in _____ to review the allegations raised in Plaintiff's claim for relief.

6. ☐ Service of Order: Plaintiff(s) shall have a disinterested third party serve a copy of this Order and the motion no later than _____on defendant(s). An Affidavit of Service MUST be filed with the court prior to the hearing.

7. ☐ Service of Order: The Clerk of Court shall either deliver in person or mail a copy of this Order by first class mail to the parties.

8. ☐ Defendant shall pay a penalty in the amount of $_____.00 within 15 days of the date of this order. If Defendant fails to do so, Plaintiff shall be entitled to have judgment entered against Defendant for any unpaid amount of this penalty by filing with the District Court an affidavit of default.

9. ☐ Defendant is ordered to comply with this order. If Defendant fails to do so, Defendant is put on notice that the court may appoint an Administrator pursuant to Minn. Stat. 504B.445 to ensure that this leased property is in compliance with all state and local laws.

Let Judgment Be Entered Accordingly

By the Court:

_____   Dated:_____

Judge

4. Emergency Tenant Remedy Action

ETRA Checklist

Emergency Tenant Remedy Actions (ETRA's) fall under Minn. Stat. 504B.381. Generally emergencies are: 1) loss of running water, 2) loss of hot water, 3) loss of heat, 4) loss of electricity, 5) loss of sanitary facilities or other essential services.

Most ETRA's are loss of water or heat.

1. ☐ On Record, state the parties present and the address of property in question. Put names of parties present in order.

2. ☐ Make sure Landlord has been properly served.

Very often Landlord has NOT been served. Ex Parte relief is not a good idea and need to get Landlord involved. Tenant is ordered to have a disinterested third party serve Landlord but they do not always do that. The Clerk of Housing Court will mail a copy of the petition to Landlord and often that is all that is needed. If Landlord is not served, you need to reschedule the hearing. You could have Tenant deposit rent with court and this usually will get the Landlord's attention. If an IFP has been filed and approved and you want to order the Sheriff to serve, be sure to schedule the hearing far enough out to allow time for the Sheriff to serve.

3. ☐ Read petition and ask Tenant if petition is true. Clarify emergency.

Most cases are loss of water or heat. These issues are pretty basic. With water case, bills are usually unpaid and with heat cases, the furnace is not working properly for some reason.

When the Minneapolis Water Utility office shuts off the water, they will send Tenants to Housing Court to address issue. When Housing Court sets an Emergency hearing, the Water Utility office will turn the water back on pending the result of the hearing once Tenant delivers a copy of the Order to them.

4. ☐ Look at a copy of the lease if one exists. Determine how much rent is and how much rent Tenant owes at time of hearing.

Most of time, there is no dispute on what rent is due. Often Tenant owes Landlord rent. If unpaid water bill, this is obvious and a quick remedy to water problem. Simply allow Tenant to pay the water bill instead of paying Landlord rent. If heat problem, you can have Tenant deposit rent with court until the heat issue resolved. This usually works.

Sometimes, the lease provides that Tenant is supposed to pay the water bill. In those cases Tenant should be ordered to pay and costs could be awarded to Landlord since Landlord has not done anything wrong.

5. ☐ Determine what needs to be done to resolve the emergency. Conduct hearing if necessary.

Often, you can figure out the problem pretty quickly. The water bill must be paid and you can order Tenant to apply their rent to the bill or order Landlord to pay it. You can assess fines and penalties also under 504B.425.

6. ☐ If necessary, schedule a compliance hearing to make sure your order is carried out.

7. ☐ Prepare Findings and Order ASAP.

State of Minnesota   **District Court**

Judicial District:
Court File Number:
Case Type: Housing

Plaintiff

ORDER ON PETITION FOR
EMERGENCY RELIEF
UNDER TENANT
REMEDIES ACT
MINNESOTA STATUTE
504B.381

vs.

Defendant

This case was heard by the undersigned on _____.
                                                                        Date

PLAINTIFF: Represented by: ☐ counsel   ☐ agent
☐ Appeared in person.
☐ Did not appear and is in default.   _____
_____   Name

DEFENDANT: Represented by: ☐ advocate   ☐ counsel
☐ Appeared in person.
☐ Did not appear and is in default.   _____
_____   Name

    Based upon the verified petition, testimony, evidence, and arguments presented, and all of the files, records, and proceedings, the Court makes the following:

FINDINGS OF FACT AND CONCLUSIONS OF LAW

1.   ☐ The property in issue is located at _____.

2.   ☐ Plaintiff(s) is/are a tenant at the property.

3. ☐ The name and address of the defendant(s) is/are

_____.

4. ☐ Defendant(s) is/are the owner(s) and/or manager(s) of the property.

5. ☐ Emergency:

a. ☐ There exists an emergency caused by the loss of utilities, facilities, or other essential services that the building owner(s) or manager(s) is/are responsible for providing, namely: _____.

b. ☐ There does not exist an emergency caused by the loss of utilities, facilities, or other essential services that the building owner(s) or manager(s) is/are responsible for providing.

6. Notice to the defendant(s):

a. ☐ Plaintiff(s) made the following reasonable attempts to notify defendant(s) that Plaintiff(s) would seek emergency relief: _____

_____

b. ☐ Plaintiff(s) did not make reasonable attempts to notify defendant(s) that Plaintiff(s) would seek emergency relief to correct the problems.

7. Actions of Plaintiff(s):

a. ☐ This emergency was **not** the result of the deliberate or negligent act or omission of Plaintiff(s) or anyone acting under Plaintiff(s)' direction or control.

b. ☐ This emergency was the result of the deliberate or negligent act or omission Plaintiff(s) or a person acting under Plaintiff(s)' direction or control.

8. The parties have reached a settlement of this matter.

9. ☐ Other: _____.

Based upon the above Findings of Fact and Conclusions of Law, the Court makes the following:

ORDER

1. ☐ Plaintiff(s)' request for emergency relief is denied.

2. ☐ Plaintiff(s)' request for emergency relief is granted as follows:

a. ☐ Defendant(s) shall take the following action to immediately correct the emergency:

_____.

b. ☐ Plaintiff(s) shall fix the problem(s) and deduct the cost up to the amount of $_____ from the rent for each of the following months:

_____.

c. ☐ An administrator shall take over operation of the property to fix the emergency problems.

d. ☐ On or before _____ Defendant(s) shall pay to Plaintiff(s) a rent refund or credit in the total amount of $_____ for the problems that existed during the month(s) of: _____.

e. ☐ Defendant(s) shall give Plaintiff(s) a future rent credit each month in the amount of $_____ until the emergency problems are fixed.

f. ☐ If Defendant(s) violates this Order, Defendant(s) shall be fined $_____.

g. ☐ On or before _____ Defendant(s) shall pay to Plaintiff(s) attorney's fees and costs in the amount of $_____.

h. ☐ On or before _____ Defendant(s) shall pay to Plaintiff(s) costs in the amount of $_____.

i. ☐ The Settlement Agreement is approved and its terms incorporated herein.

3. ☐ This matter is scheduled for a hearing on _____ at _____ ____.m. in _____ to review the allegations raised in Plaintiff's claim for relief.

4. ☐ PARTIES ARE ORDERED TO BRING TO THE COURT HEARING COPIES OF LEASE FOR THIS RENTAL PROPERTY AND VERIFICATION OF RENT PAID OR RENT DUE.

5. ☐ RENT INTO COURT: Plaintiff shall pay into court the rent **of** $_____**.00** in cash or certified funds payable to the Court Administrator, on or before _____ **at** (_____), or the Court will dismiss Plaintiff's petition for relief and the hearing scheduled in this order shall be cancelled.

6.   ☐ Service of Order: Plaintiff(s) shall have a disinterested third party serve a copy of this Order and the motion no later than _____on defendant(s).   An Affidavit of Service MUST be filed with the court prior to the hearing.

7.   ☐ Service of Order: The Clerk of Court shall either deliver in person or mail a copy of this Order by first class mail to the parties.

Let Judgment Be Entered Accordingly

By the Court:

_____   Dated:_____

Judge

5. Unlawful Lockout Checklist

Lockout Checklist

Unlawful residential lockout, exclusion, or removals fall under Minn. Stat. 504B.375. Lockouts can be actual (change locks) or constructive (remove door or termination of utilities). This **does not apply to commercial property**.

1. ☐ On Record, state the parties present and the address of property in question. Put names of parties present in order.

Often names are misspelled or even wrong parties named. This needs to be clarified.

2. ☐ Make sure Landlord has been properly served.

Very often Landlord has NOT been served.   Ex Parte relief not a good idea and need to get Landlord involved.   Tenant is ordered to have a disinterested third party serve Landlord but they do not always do that. The Clerk of Housing Court will mail a copy of the petition to Landlord and often that is all that is needed. If Landlord not served, you need to reschedule hearing.

3. ☐ Read petition and ask Tenant if petition true. Clarify details of lockout. Clarify what Tenant wants.

You need to verify somehow that Tenant is actually a Tenant at the leased property. Often Tenant's do not have their lease because they say it is locked in the property. Need driver's license, copies of bills, or some other way to confirm that Tenant is indeed a Tenant at leased property. Sometimes all Tenant wants is to get access to leased property to retrieve their personal belongings.

4. ☐ Look at a copy of the lease if one exists. Determine how much rent is and how much rent Tenant owes at time of hearing. In short, you must make sure person who filed complaint is actually a tenant!

Most of time, Tenant owes rent and that is why Landlord locked him/her out.   Landlord cannot do this without agreement made at time of lock change or filing an eviction action. If person who filed is not a residential Tenant as defined in Minn. Stat. 504B, then no relief available. Also, no relief if parties not Landlord and Tenant (e.g. roommates or Husband and Wife).

5. ☐ Determine whether alleged lockout is improper under Minn. Stat. 504B.375. Conduct hearing if necessary.

*Often, you can figure out the issue pretty quickly. You can assess costs and order rent abatement if appropriate. **Damages for ouster are set forth in Minn. Stat. 504B.231. May award attorney fees.***

6. ☐ If necessary, schedule a compliance hearing to make sure your order is carried out.

7. ☐ Prepare Findings and Order ASAP.

Housing Court cases are summary proceedings and it is important to get orders out as soon as possible. Orders should give specific findings.

8. ☐ Costs.

State of Minnesota	**District Court**
	Judicial District:
	Court File Number:
	Case Type: Housing

_____

Plaintiff

ORDER ON PETITION FOR POSSESSION OF RESIDENTIAL RENTAL PROPERTY FOLLOWING UNLAWFUL REMOVAL OR EXCLUSION UNDER MINNESOTA STATUTE 504B.375

vs.

_____

Defendant

_____

This case was heard by the undersigned on _____.
Date

PLAINTIFF: Represented by: ☐ counsel   ☐ agent
☐ Appeared in person.
☐ Did not appear and is in default.   _____
Name

DEFENDANT: Represented by: ☐ advocate   ☐ counsel
☐ Appeared in person.
☐ Did not appear and is in default.   _____
Name

      Based upon the verified petition, testimony, evidence, and arguments presented, and all of the files, records, and proceedings, the Court makes the following:

FINDINGS OF FACT AND CONCLUSIONS OF LAW

1. ☐ The property in issue is located at _____.

2. ☐ Plaintiff(s) is/are a residential tenant at the property.

3. ☐ The name and address of the defendant(s) is/are _____

_____.

4. ☐   Defendant(s) is/are the owner(s) and/or manager(s) of the property.

5. ☐   Landlord(s) actually or constructively and unlawfully removed or excluded Tenant(s) from the property by taking the following action: _____
_____.

6. ☐   Landlord(s) did not actually or constructively and unlawfully remove or exclude plaintiff(s) from the property.

7. ☐   The court has not issued an eviction judgment and writ of recovery in favor of Landlord(s) and against Tenant(s), or the court has issued an eviction judgment and writ of recovery in favor of Landlord(s) and against the Tenant(s) but Landlord(s) did not execute it lawfully.

8. ☐   The court issued an eviction judgment and writ of recovery in favor of Landlord(s) and against Tenant(s), and Landlord(s) executed it lawfully.

9. ☐   Tenant(s) is/are able to pay monetary security.

10. In unlawful lockouts or unlawful exclusion of property, Tenant may be entitled to the following relief under Minnesota Law:

a.   Treble damages or $500.00 whichever is greater, and reasonable attorneys fees under Minn. Stat. 504B.231.

b.   A civil penalty of up to $300.00, actual damages and attorney fees under Minn. Stat. 504B.271.

Based upon the foregoing Findings of Fact and Conclusions of Law, the court makes the following:

ORDER

1. ☐ Tenant(s)' request for relief is denied.

2. ☐ Tenant(s)' request for relief is granted as follows:

☐ a. Landlord(s) shall allow Tenant(s) to immediately move back into the property.

☐ b. Landlord(s) shall allow Tenant(s) to have sufficient access to the property to move out his/her/their belongings.

☐ c. Landlord(s) shall immediately stop the unlawful actions that are keeping Tenant(s) out of the property.

☐ d. The Sheriff of this County shall execute and enforce this Order by

> (1) making a demand upon Landlord(s) or other person in charge of the premises to take the action ordered by the Court;

> (2) taking whatever action may be necessary to cause the action ordered of the Landlord(s) by the Court to be taken immediately, including putting Tenant back in possession and making property secure for Tenant. After the Sheriff or a Deputy Sheriff has made a public demand which has been refused or to which no response has been made, the Sheriff or his Deputy is authorized to cause the building or enclosure to be broken open to take the action ordered by the Court.

> (3) In the event that the Sheriff or a Deputy sheriff is required to cause the building or enclosure to be broken open to take the action ordered by the Court, neither the Sheriff, Deputy Sheriff, Hennepin County, State of Minnesota, nor any person or entity hired or retained by the Sheriff or the Deputy to assist the Deputy in effecting this Order shall be liable for any damages resulting there from.

> (4) All fees and costs associated with the performance of the duties required by this Order, including service fees of the Sheriff, shall be borne by the Landlord. Landlord may request a court hearing to contest any fees and costs assessed by filing a motion before this Court.

3. ☐ Penalty:

On or before _____, Landlord(s) shall pay to Tenant(s) the amount of $_____ as a penalty for the unlawful lockout. In the event Landlord does not make this payment, then upon filing of an affidavit of default by Tenant, a judgment shall be entered in favor of Tenant against Landlord, together with all costs and disbursements incurred by Tenant, including the $200.00 allowed by Minn. Stat. 549.02.

4. ☐ Service of Order: Tenant(s) shall have a disinterested third party serve a copy of this Order and the motion no later than _____ on defendant(s) and provide an affidavit of service to the court to verify this service.

5. ☐ The Clerk of Court shall either give to the parties or mail to the parties by first class mail a copy of this Order.

6. ☐ The Sheriff shall serve this Order and the Verified Petition upon defendant(s) at no cost to Tenant(s).

7. ☐ Other relief: _____ _____.

8. This matter is continued until _____, at _____ o'clock am/pm in courtroom _____ for further hearing.

Let Judgment Be Entered Accordingly

By the Court:

_____   Dated:_____

Judge

6. Motion to Quash Writ Checklist

Motion to Quash Checklist

Motions to Quash writs are basically Rule 60 motions for relief from an order due to fraud, mistake, etc. Most of time, motions are made asking for more time to make payment due or alleging that in fact payment was made. A deposit may be required before the Court will allow motion hearing to be held.

1. ☐ Review names of parties and address of property in question. Make sure writ has not yet been executed.

Motion is moot if Writ has already been executed. If Writ has not yet been executed you may proceed.

2. ☐ Make sure Tenant has made reasonable attempts to notify Landlord of motion.

3. ☐ Review motion. Schedule motion hearing as soon as possible if necessary. Require deposit of all money due prior to the hearing to ensure no prejudice.

In most cases, Tenants are asking for more time to make a payment to redeem the tenancy or simply want more time to move out. Note: The Court of Appeals in an unpublished opinion has held that the Court can refuse the Tenant any further relief if Tenant fails to redeem at or before the exact time and date ordered.[10] Sometimes Tenant alleges Landlord refused to take the rent money. In those cases you can have Tenant deposit the rent with the court and stay the Writ pending a hearing.

4. ☐ Prepare Findings and Order and order Tenant to serve Landlord notice of motion.

Housing Court cases are summary proceedings and it is important to get orders out as soon as possible. Orders should give specific findings.

---

[10] STATE OF MINNESOTAIN COURT OF APPEALS (unpublished opinion) C4-02-1239 **Paul Jasa, etal.,vs.LaMac Cleaners, Inc.**, Filed January 28, 2003. (Held that Tenant attempt to redeem property by paying amount ordered 10 minutes late was not valid. In order for a Tenant to redeem, the Tenant must pay the money ordered in a timely manner and being 10 minutes late was "not in a timely manner".

State of Minnesota | **District Court**

Judicial District:
Court File Number:
Case Type: Housing

_____

Plaintiff

ORDER

vs.

_____

Defendant

_____

This case was heard by the undersigned on _____.
Date

PLAINTIFF: Represented by: ☐ counsel   ☐
agent
☐ Appeared in person.
☐ Did not appear and is in default.   _____
_____   Name

DEFENDANT: Represented by: ☐ advocate   ☐
counsel
☐ Appeared in person.
☐ Did not appear and is in default.   _____
                                                                                     Name

Based upon the verified petition, testimony, evidence, and arguments presented, and all of the files, records, and proceedings, the Court makes the following:

Findings Of Fact And Conclusions Of Law

1. A Writ of Recovery was issued in this matter on _____. The property address is: _____.

2. Tenant claims the Writ of Recovery should be quashed because:

_____.

3. Other finding(s): _____.

Order

☐ 1. The Writ of Recovery issued in this matter is hereby quashed and the previously entered Judgment for the Writ is vacated.

☐ 2. Tenant's motion to quash the Writ of Recovery is hereby DENIED. The stay is lifted and the Writ of Recovery is reinstated and may be executed immediately.

☐ 3. Execution of the Writ of Recovery issued in this matter shall be stayed temporarily pending the hearing scheduled below upon Tenant depositing with court in cash or certified funds payable to the Court Administrator the amount of $ _____, PROVIDED THAT Tenant deposits this money no later than _____ at 2:00 p.m.

☐ 4. HEARING: This is scheduled for a court hearing on _____, at _____.m. Both parties shall come to _____ for courtroom assignment.

☐ 5. If Tenant fails to deposit any funds ordered above, then this hearing shall be cancelled and the stay on the writ shall be lifted.

☐ 6. SERVICE OF ORDER: The Clerk of Court shall either give to the parties or mail to the parties by first class mail a copy of this Order.

☐ 7. Defendant(s) shall have a disinterested third party serve a copy of this order and the motion no later than _____ on Plaintiff(s). An Affidavit of Service MUST be filed with the court prior to the hearing.

Let Judgment Be Entered Accordingly

By the Court:

Dated:_____

_____
Judge

7. Expungement Checklist

Expungement Checklist

Motions to expunge Housing Court files are authorized under Minn. Stat. 484.014 [11]. Expungement motions should be in writing and signed by the Tenant.[12] The issue in expungement motions is whether Landlord's case was sufficiently without basis in fact or law, which may include lack of jurisdiction over the case. The court must find that expungement is clearly in the interests of justice and those interests are not outweighed by the public's interest in knowing about the record.[13] In certain cases involving mortgage foreclosures, mandatory expungement is required if the Tenant vacated prior to the commencement of the eviction action or did not receive notice required by Minn. Stat. 504B.285.

1. ☐ On Record, state the parties present and the address of property in question. Put names of parties present in order.

---

[11] **484.014 Housing records; expungement of eviction information.**

Subdivision 1. **Definitions.** For the purpose of this section, the following terms have the meanings given:

(1) "expungement" means the removal of evidence of the court file's existence from the publicly accessible records;

(2) "eviction case" means an action brought under sections 504B.281 to 504B.371; and

(3) "court file" means the court file created when an eviction case is filed with the court.

Subd. 2. **Discretionary expungement.** The court may order expungement of an eviction case court file only upon **motion** of a defendant and decision by the court, if the court finds that the plaintiff's case is sufficiently without basis in fact or law, which may include lack of jurisdiction over the case, that expungement is clearly in the interests of justice and those interests are not outweighed by the public's interest in knowing about the record.

Subd. 3. **Mandatory expungement.** The court shall order expungement of an eviction case commenced solely on the grounds provided in section 504B.285, subdivision 1, clause (1), if the court finds that the defendant occupied real property that was subject to contract for deed cancellation or mortgage foreclosure and: (1) the time for contract cancellation or foreclosure redemption has expired and the defendant vacated the property prior to commencement of the eviction action; or (2) the defendant was a tenant during the contract cancellation or foreclosure redemption period and did not receive a notice under section 504B.285, subdivision 1a, 1b, or 1c, to vacate on a date prior to commencement of the eviction case.

[12] Rule 7.02 of Rules of Civil procedure says a motion, unless made during the hearing or trial, shall be in writing

[13] There is a public right to know issue here. Landlord and Tenants used to make deals and Landlords would get tenants out without fight by agreeing to expungement. Other Landlords unhappy with this. Must balance interests.

2. ☐ Make sure Landlord has been properly served. *(Note: Rule 6.04 of the Rules of Civil Procedure requires 5 days for service of motion. Since under Rule 6.01 Saturdays and Sundays are excluded in the 5 days, the best practice is to simply require 7 days notice, and 10 days if notice is by mail since under rule 6.05 3 days should be added if service is by mail).*

3. ☐ Determine facts. Conduct hearing. Was eviction without basis in fact or law? *There are basically three parties to every Expungement case. The Landlord, the Tenant and the Public. Good expungement cases are a) bad or no service b) Landlord admits mistake made and case should not have been brought, and c) Tenant renting from a owner in foreclosed property and is being evicted because of foreclosure.*

4. ☐ Prepare Findings and Order ASAP. Remember, do not expunge a case if there is anything else that needs to be done on the file.

More Expungement Info

1. Current Hennepin County Housing Court policy when a file is ordered expunged:

> a) File is given to the Housing Court Leadworker.
>
> b) Order is reviewed to ensure expungement was ordered. The appeal time is 10 days. Wait 14 days from the order date to do the physical expungement unless case is appealed.
>
> c) Case information is entered into a database.
>
> d) Case is expunged from MNCIS.
>
> e) A form reading "Expunged & Sealed" is attached to the front of the file.
>
> f) The physical file is destroyed.

2. Under Blacks Law Dictionary, the definition of Expungement is to "obliterate", "to strike out wholly" to "destroy".

3. Nothing further can happen on a case if it is expunged! This means no further action, no judgments, no further reference to file and arguably, no "Res Judicata" *(this is disputed by some lawyers and there may be an issue here).* This means that if a

Judicial Officer expunges a file that nothing further should be done on that file unless appealed.

4. If a party wants a case expunged, they should wait until nothing further needs to be done on the file before asking that it be expunged.

State of Minnesota   **District Court**

| Judicial District: |
| Court File Number: |
| Case Type: Housing |

_____

Plaintiff

EXPUNGEMENT ORDER

vs.

_____

Defendant

_____

This case was heard by the undersigned on _____.

Date

PLAINTIFF: Represented by: ☐ counsel   ☐ agent
☐ Appeared in person.
☐ Did not appear and is in default.   _____

_____   Name

DEFENDANT: Represented by: ☐ advocate   ☐ counsel
☐ Appeared in person.
☐ Did not appear and is in default.   _____

                                                                     Name

     Based upon the verified petition, testimony, evidence, and arguments presented, and all of the files, records, and proceedings, the Court makes the following:

<u>FINDINGS OF FACT AND CONCLUSIONS OF LAW</u>

     1. ☐ The moving party has proven by a preponderance of the evidence that the landlord's case was without sufficient basis in law or fact and expungement is clearly in the interests of justice and the interests of justice are not outweighed by the public's interest in knowing about the record.

     2. ☐ The moving party has failed to prove that expungement is warranted under Minn. Stat. § 484.014.

     3. ☐ That the Order Setting Motion for Expungement provides: "3. That the moving party file Affidavits of Service with the District Court Administrator by 3:00 p.m.,

three days prior to the hearing. Failure to file these documents in a timely manner will be cause to strike the hearing." That the moving party has not complied with this order and the motion is summarily dismissed.

ORDER

1. ☐ The Court Administrator shall expunge court file _____ by removing evidence of the court file's existence from the publicly accessible records.

2. ☐ The Court Administrator shall expunge _____ from the record by removing evidence of that party's name from the publicly accessible records.

3. ☐ The motion to expunge is dismissed with_____ prejudice.

4. ☐ The motion to expunge is denied.

5. ☐ Other_____.

Let Judgment Be Entered Accordingly

By the Court:

_____   Dated:_____

Judge

8. Settlement Form

The settlement form on the following page can be found at the Minnesota
Judicial Branch Website at www.mncourts.gov.

State of Minnesota   **District Court**

County	Judicial District: _____
	Court File Number: _____
	Case Type: Housing

Name of Plaintiff(s)

vs   **SETTLEMENT AGREEMENT**

Name of Defendant(s)

The parties have reached the following agreement:

_____

☐   Parties agree to the following payment schedule:

Date Payment is Due	Time Due (if applicable)	Amount Due	Form of Payment (Money Order, Certified Funds, etc.)
/ /	AM / PM		
/ /	AM / PM		
/ /	AM / PM		
/ /	AM / PM		
/ /	AM / PM		

☐   No Writ of Recovery is requested at this time. This signed agreement serves as settlement.

☐   Defendant(s) shall vacate on or before _____ or a Writ of Recovery shall be issued upon request of Plaintiff and payment of the fee for a Writ. There will be no notice to Defendant or hearing.

☐   If any payment is missed or other terms of the settlement are violated, a Writ of Recovery shall be issued upon request by Plaintiff and payment of the fee, and filing of an affidavit stating how the agreement was violated. There will be no notice to Defendant or hearing. A request for the Writ must be made within 30 days of the violation of the agreement.

☐   If a Writ of Recovery issues, Plaintiff may file an affidavit requesting costs and disbursements allowed by statute, and the court shall award a judgment against Defendant for allowable costs and disbursements.

I have read, understand, and agree to be bound by this Settlement Agreement:

_____   _____

PRINT Plaintiff'(s) **NAME**   **PRINT** Defendant'(s) **NAME**

_____   _____

SIGNATURE OF OWNER/AGENT/ATTORNEY   SIGNATURE

Date _____   Date _____

9. Housing Court Issues

See Index of Housing Court Issues at end of book.

Housing court Issues and Caselaw

1. Abandonment.   Personal Property.

Minn. Stat. 504B.271 allows a Landlord to take possession of Tenants personal property if a Tenant abandons the rented premises. Landlord must care and store the property for 28 days (*2010 law which takes effect 08/01/2010*).   Landlord must allow the Tenant to recover the personal property after payment of the costs of removal, care and storage of the personal property.

Minnesota law provides that a tenant illegally removed or excluded from the possession of leased premises has an action under Minn. Stat. § 504B.375.   Minn. Stat. § 504B.375, (*in association with Minn. Stat. §§ 504B.225 and 504B.231*) penalizes landlords who unlawfully exclude tenants from residential premises.   **A defense to wrongful exclusion is abandonment.**

Abandonment requires conduct and intent, *i.e.*, both the voluntary relinquishment of possession and an intent to relinquish possession. *State v. McCoy*, 228 Minn. 420, 422, 38 N.W.2d 386, 388 (1949).   Intention is essential to a determination of whether abandonment has occurred. *Rowe v. City of Minneapolis*, 49 Minn. 148, 157, 51 N.W. 907, 908 (1892).

The intent to abandon "need not appear by express declaration, buy may be shown by acts and conduct clearly inconsistent with an intention to continue the use of the property for the purposes for which it was acquired" *Richards Asphalt Co. v. Bunge Corp.* 399 N.W.2d 188, 192 (Minn. App. 1987) and *Norton v. Duluth Transfer Ry. Co.*, 151 N.W. 907, 909 (Minn. 1915).

The penalty to Landlords who wrongfully retains Tenants personal property or refuses to return the property to Tenant within 24-48 hours after Tenant gives notice as set forth in the statute has been increased to twice the actual damages or $1,000.00, whichever is greater (effective 08/01/2010).

Minn. Stat. 504B.365 state that the District Court hearing the eviction action retains jurisdiction to hear matters involving 504B.271 personal property issues.   Law states that if Landlord refused to return property after proper demand made, the District Court can order relief including damages, expenses and attorney fees.

2. Absurd Results

Minn. Statutes 645.17 Presumptions in Ascertaining Legislative Intent

In ascertaining the intention of the legislature the courts may be guided by the following presumptions:

> (1) the legislature does not intend a result that is absurd, impossible of execution, or unreasonable;
> (2) the legislature intends the entire statute to be effective and certain;
> (3) the legislature does not intend to violate the Constitution of the United States or of this state;
> (4) when a court of last resort has construed the language of a law, the legislature in subsequent laws on the same subject matter intends the same construction to be placed upon such language; and
> (5) the legislature intends to favor the public interest as against any private interest.

3. Address of Landlord on Rental Application

Minn. Stat. 504B.181 requires disclosure to Tenants in the rental agreement or prior to commencement of the tenancy the name and address of the person authorized to manage the premises and the Landlord or agent authorized to accept service of process. Under 504B.181, this information must be posted on the property in a conspicuous place on the premises.   Subdivision 4 of this statute states that the Landlord cannot bring an action against Tenant unless the name and address has **either been known** by or disclosed to the Tenant at least 30 days prior to the initiation of any action. This suggests proof of actual notice by Tenant of Landlord's name or agent and address may satisfy this requirement of the statute.

The most certain means of contacting a property owner is through his residence address, not his post office box or telephone number. By providing a residence address, the city can contact the property owner immediately, even if telephone lines are down, the property owner has changed his telephone number, or the property owner has refused to answer the telephone. Furthermore, first-class mail takes at least one day to be delivered.   If a property owner does not check his mail on a regular basis, many days could pass before the city would succeed in contacting the property owner.   In light of the foregoing scenarios, The Court of Appeals has held that requiring a residence address on a **rental license** application is rationally related to a legitimate governmental interest. *City of Minneapolis vs. Thomas A. Swansion (C.A. file No. C5-97-312) 1997 (unpublished case).*

The city of Minneapolis, (*Code of Ordinances* § 244.1840, 1991) requires a property owner's residence address on a **rental license** application and specifically prohibits the use of a post office box as an address.

4. Affirmative Defenses

Minn. Stat. 504B.335 provides that at the initial court appearance specified in the summons, the Defendant may answer the complaint, and the court shall hear and decide the action, unless it grants a continuance of the trial as provided in Minn. Stat. 504B.341.

The Minnesota Rules of Civil Procedure in Rule 8.03 provides that a party must set forth in an answer or pleading all affirmative defenses, which includes waiver, bankruptcy, accord and satisfaction, etc. This rule implies that affirmative defenses must be plead in an answer. Rule 8.04 provides that "Averments in a pleading to which responsive pleading is required....are admitted when not denied in the responsive pleading." "Averments in a pleading to which no responsive pleading is required or permitted shall be taken as denied or avoided."

Answers are NOT required to be filed in an Eviction Action. Failure to file an Answer constitutes a general denial to the complaint. Affirmative defenses MUST be affirmatively pled and therefore Defendant should file a written Answer whenever an affirmative defense is being asserted.

5. Appeals

1. Basic Fact Scenerio

Tenant has filed a notice of Appeal of an order which either granted possession of leased property to Landlord or allowed the Tenant the right to redeem his/her tenancy by paying to Landlord an amount determined by the Court owed by Tenant to bring her rent payments current.

2. Appeal Process

A party who feels aggrieved by the judgment may appeal within **ten days** as provided for civil actions in district court. See Minn. Stat. 504B.371. Appeals may be made to the court of Appeals as allowed by Minn. Stat. 504B.371 or in Hennepin and Ramsey Counties may be to a Judge as allowed by Housing Court Rules 611.

3. Rules and Statutes regarding the Appeal or Supercedeas Bond

There are three different places that you can go to review rules and guidelines regarding setting a supercedeas bond. There are Housing Court Rule 611, Minn. Rules of Civil Appeallate Procedure Rule 108 and Minnesota Statutes 504B.371.

a. **Housing Court Rule 611** states as follows:

> *(b) Stays.* In civil cases, filing and service of a notice of review does not stay entry of judgment nor vacate a judgment if already entered unless the petitioner requests and the referee orders a bond, payment(s) in lieu of a bond, or waiver of bond and payment(s). The decision to set or waive a bond or payment(s) in lieu of bond shall be based upon Minn. R. Civ. App. P. 108, subdivisions 1 & 5. A hearing on a bond or payment(s) in lieu of bond shall be scheduled before the referee, and the referee's order shall remain in effect unless a judge modifies or vacates the order.

b. **Minn. Rule of Civ App. P. 108 subdivisions 1 & 5** state as follows (2008 version):

> *Subd 1. Effect of Appeal; Stay.* Except in appeals under Rule 103.03 (b), or as otherwise provided by law, the filing of a proper and timely appeal suspends the authority of the trial court to make any order necessarily affecting the order or judgment appealed from. The trial court retains jurisdiction as to matters independent of, supplemental to, or collateral to the order or judgment appealed from, and to enforce its order or judgment.
>
> Unless otherwise provided by law, a proper and timely appeal does not stay an order or judgment or enforcement proceedings in the trial court, but the appellant may obtain a stay by providing a supersedeas bond or other security in the amount and form which the trial court shall order and approve, in the cases provided in this rule, or as otherwise provided by rule or statute.
>
> An application to approve a supersedeas bond, or for a stay on other terms, shall be made in the first instance to the trial court. Upon motion, the appellate court may review the trial court's determination as to whether a stay is appropriate and the terms of any stay.
>
> A supersedeas bond, whether approved by the trial court or appellate court, shall be filed in the trial court.
>
> *Subd. 5.* If the appeal is from a judgment directing the sale or delivery of possession of real property, the condition of the bond shall be the payment of the value of the use and occupation of the property from the time of the appeal until the delivery of possession of the property if the judgment is affirmed and the undertaking that the appellant shall not commit or suffer the commission of any waste on the property while it remains in the appellant's possession during the pendency of the appeal.

c. **Minnesota Statute 504B.371** states as follows:

> ***Subd 3: Appeal bond.*** *If the party appealing remains in possession of the property, that party must give a bond that provides that:*
>
> > *(i) all costs of the appeal will be paid;*
> >
> > *(ii) the party will comply with the court's order; and*
> >
> > *(iii) all rent and other damages due to the party excluded from possession during the pendency of the appeal will be paid.*

The Court of Appeals Decision *Camber Hill Limited Partnership dba Camber Hill Townhomes vs. Edward Samuel and John Doe, et. al. (Court of Appeals A06-6, (unpublished 2006)* addressed the issue of setting a bond pending an appeal in a Housing Court case. The Court of Appeals in that decision made the following statement:

> *Rule 108.01, subd 5, addresses stays pending appeal in cases directing sale or delivery of possession of real property, generally. It is Minn. Stat. 504B.371, subd 3 (2004), however, that addresses stays pending appeal in eviction matters, specifically. And the district court did not address or apply this statute. Under it, a party remaining in possession of the premises pending appeal is to assure the district court that, among other things, "all rent and other damages due to the party excluded from possession during the pendency of the appeal will be paid." Id at subd. 3(3). Therefore, the district court's order, which does not require appellant to post any financial security or show that financial security was unnecessary to protect respondent, has not satisfied Minn. Stat. 504B.371, subd. 3. Cf County of Blue Earth v. Wingen 684 N.W. 2d 919 (Minn. App. 2004) (stating "the purpose of supersedeas bond conditions is to assure that, pending the outcome of an appeal, the economic risk of the appeal is not borne by the party that prevailed below."*

If the party appealing remains in possession of the premises, that party must give a bond to **"ensure that the economic risk of the appeal** is not borne by the party that prevailed below". In addition, the bond should ensure as required in Minn. Stat. 504B.371 subd. 3 that **"all rent and other damages due to the party** excluded from the possession during the pendency of the appeal will be paid." The only way to ensure that all rent and other damages due to Landlord as set forth in the order are paid is to have Tenant deposit this amount as part of the supercedeas bond. Otherwise, if the only amount Tenant has to pay is the ongoing rent, Tenant has in effect extended the term of the lease to the detriment of Landlord. The result could be that Tenant gets more time in the leased property and Landlord has no assurances that Tenant will pay the amount ordered by the trial court as a result of the trial. This would be requiring the prevailing party to bear the economic risk of the appeal which is contrary to Minn. Stat. 504B.371.

d. Appeal Bond where there has been foreclosure.

Minn. Stat. 580.28 (see below)[14] sets forth a procedure where if the mortgagor claims that a mortgage is fraudulent or void the mortgagor may deposit with the Sheriff an amount for which the mortgaged premises were sold, plus interest (the redemption amount). This statute states that such foreclosure, deposit, bond, and notice shall be brought to the attention of the court by supplemental complaint in the action. The court by judgment shall determine the validity of the foreclosure sale, and the rights of the parties to the moneys and bond so deposited.

Attorneys representing Banks therefore argue, that if a person in possession of property alleges the mortgage was fraudulent or void and seeks a judicial or appellate review of an order awarding possession based on this claim, they should deposit as a bond the redemption amount which would equal the amount bid at sale plus interest.

The amount of a bond posted on an appeal in foreclosure cases, therefore, may vary depending on whether or not the person in possession is a tenant or a mortgagor asserting a void or fraudulent mortgage.

---

[14] *Minn.Stat. 580.28- Action to Set Aside Mortgage; Foreclosure; Redemption.* When an action is brought wherein it is claimed that any mortgage as to the plaintiff or person for whose benefit the action is brought is fraudulent or void, or has been paid or discharged, in whole or in part, or the relative priority or the validity of liens is disputed, if such mortgage has been foreclosed by advertisement, and the time for redemption from the foreclosure sale will expire before final judgment in such action, the plaintiff or beneficiary having the right to redeem, for the purpose of saving such right in case the action fails, **may deposit with the sheriff before the time of redemption expires the amount for which the mortgaged premises were sold, with interest thereon to the time of deposit, together with a bond to the holder of the sheriff's certificate of sale,** in an amount and with sureties to be approved by the sheriff, conditioned to pay all interest that may accrue or be allowed on such deposit if the action fail. The person shall, in writing, notify such sheriff that the person claims the mortgage to be fraudulent or void, or to have been paid or discharged, in whole or in part, as the case may be, and that such action is pending, and direct the sheriff to retain such money and bond until final judgment. In case such action fails, such deposit shall operate as a redemption of the premises from such foreclosure sale, and entitle the plaintiff to a certificate thereof. Such foreclosure, deposit, bond, and notice shall be brought to the attention of the court by supplemental complaint in the action, and the judgment shall determine the validity of the foreclosure sale, and the rights of the parties to the moneys and bond so deposited, which shall be paid and delivered by the sheriff as directed by such judgment upon delivery to the sheriff of a certified copy thereof. The remedy herein provided shall be in addition to other remedies now existing. (2011)

6. Attorneys Fees.

If a residential lease specifies an action, circumstances, or an extent to which a landlord, directly, or through additional rent, may recover attorney fees in an action between the landlord and tenant, the tenant is entitled to attorney fees if the tenant prevails in the same type of action, under the same circumstances, and to the same extent as specified in the lease for the landlord. (Minn. Stat. 504B.172).

Minn. Stat. 504B.172 is effective for leases entered into on or after August 1, 2011, and for leases renewed on or after August 1, 2012.

There is also an Attorney's fees provision in Minn. Stat. 504B.291 which provides that in an Action to recover possession of leased property for nonpayment of rent only (this does not apply if Landlord also alleging other material breachs of lease) the tenant has a right to redeem the tenancy by paying to the landlord or bringing to court the amount of the rent that is in arrears, with interest, costs of the action, and an attorney's fee not to exceed $5, and by performing any other covenants of the lease. This provision applies to both residential and commercial property. This means a Tenant can remain in possession by only paying $5.00 in attorney's fees, irrespective of whether or not under the lease Tenant owes Landlord attorney's fees that exceed that. The Landlord would have to sue the Tenant for these fees in a separate action.

Attorney fees are allowed under at least eleven sections under Minnesota Statutes 504B.

a. An action may be brought for willful and malicious destruction of leased residential rental property under Minn. Stat. 504B.165. The prevailing party may recover actual damages, costs, and **reasonable attorney fees**, as well as other equitable relief as determined by the court.

b. If a residential lease specifies an action, circumstances, or an extent to which a landlord, directly, or through additional rent, may recover attorney fees in an action between the landlord and tenant, the tenant is entitled to attorney fees if the tenant prevails in the same type of action, under the same circumstances, and to the same extent as specified in the lease for the landlord (Minn. Stat. 504B.172).

c. A landlord who violates Minn. Stat. 504B.173 (pertaining to Applicant Screening fees) is liable to the applicant for the application applicant screening fee plus a civil penalty of up to $100, civil court filing costs, and **reasonable attorney fees** incurred to enforce this remedy. (b) A prospective tenant who provides materially false information on the application or omits material information requested is liable to the landlord for damages, plus a civil penalty of up to $500, civil court filing costs, and **reasonable attorney fees.**

d. Minn. Stat. 504B.204 provides that a landlord, agent, or person acting under the landlord's direction or control may not accept rent or a security deposit for residential rental property from a tenant after the leased premises have been condemned or declared unfit for human habitation by the applicable state or local authority, if the tenancy commenced after the premises were condemned or declared unfit for human habitation. If a landlord, agent, or a person acting under the landlord's direction or control violates this section, the landlord is liable to the tenant for actual damages and an amount equal to three times the amount of all money collected from the tenant after date of condemnation or declaration, plus costs and **attorney fees.**

e. Under Minn. Stat. 504B.205, a Tenant has the right to seek police and emergency assistance and Landlords are prohibited from baring or limiting Tenants right to do so. A residential tenant may bring a civil action for a violation of this section and recover from the landlord $250 or actual damages, whichever is greater, and **reasonable attorney's fees.**

f. If Landlord unlawfully terminates utilities at leased property, Tenant could be entitled to treble damages, or $500.00, whichever is greater, plus reasonable **attorneys fees** (Minn. Stat. 504B.221).

g. If a landlord, an agent, or other person acting under the landlord's direction or control unlawfully and in bad faith removes, excludes, or forcibly keeps out a tenant from residential premises, the tenant may recover from the landlord treble damages or $500, whichever is greater, and **reasonable attorney's fees.** (Minn. Stat. 504B.231).

h. Tenant may redeem tenancy by paying Landlord past rent due, costs and Attorneys fees not to exceed $5.00. (Minn. Stat. 504B.291)

i. If Landlord refused to return personal property to Tenant after proper demand made, the court can order relief including damages, expenses and **attorney fees** (Minn. Stat. 504B.271 and Minn. Stat. 504B.365 subd 4).

j. If a Tenant wrongfully petitions the court for possession of property under Minn. Stat. 504B.375 alleging wrongful exclusion, the court may, upon dissolution of the order granting possession, assess costs against the residential tenant, subject to the provisions of section 563.01, and may allow damages and **reasonable attorney fees** for the wrongful granting of the order for possession.

k.   In Minn. Stat. 504B.425 subd. (g), The court may grant any relief it deems just and proper, including a judgment against the landlord for **reasonable attorney fees**, not to exceed $500, in the case of a prevailing residential tenant or neighborhood organization. The $500 limitation does not apply to awards made under section 549.211 or other specific statutory authority.

7. Attorneys in Housing Court.

In Hennepin and Ramsey Counties, Housing Court Rule 603 governs the issue of agents representing parties. The rule states as follows:

Rule 603. Parties
An unlawful detainer action shall be brought in the name of the owner of the property or other person entitled to possession of the premises. No agent shall sue in the agent's own name. Any agent suing for a principal shall attach a copy of the Power of Authority to the complaint at the time of filing. No person other than a principal or a duly licensed lawyer shall be allowed to appear in Housing Court unless the Power of Authority is attached to the complaint at the time of filing, and no person other than a duly licensed lawyer shall be allowed to appear unless the Power of Authority is so attached to the complaint. An agent or lay advocate may appear without a written Power of Authority if the party being so represented is an individual and is also present at the hearing.

A recent unpublished Court of Appeals case, namely, Walnut Towers, Respondent, vs. Lori A. Schwan, Appellant. Filed September 16, 2008 Reversed Hudson, Judge Blue Earth County District Court File No. 07-CV-07-1183 ruled that Attorneys must represent corporations in District Court in Housing Cases. This case did not address Minn. Stat. 481.02 nor did it disallow the practice in Hennepin County Housing Court to allow agents to appear for corporations under Rule 603 of the Housing Court Rules.

Clearly, under Rule 603, an agent has the right to appear for a principal and this agent does not have to be a licensed attorney so long as a Power of Authority is attached to the complaint.   However, Rule 603 states that a Power of Authority does not have to be attached to the complaint if the party is an individual.   This exception for individuals implies that agents may appear for artificial persons.

For all other counties, Minnesota Statutes 481.02 allows agents to appear in Housing Court. Minn. Stat. 481.02 (subd. 1) states as follows:

Subdivision 1.   Prohibitions. It shall be unlawful for any person or association of persons, except members of the bar of Minnesota admitted and licensed to practice as attorneys at law, to appear as attorney or counselor at law in any action or proceeding in any court in this state to maintain, conduct, or defend the same, except personally as a party thereto in other than a representative capacity, or, by word, sign, letter, or advertisement, to hold out as competent or qualified to give legal advice or counsel, or to prepare legal documents, or as being engaged in advising or counseling in law or acting as attorney or counselor at law, or in furnishing to others the services of a lawyer or lawyers, or, for a fee or any consideration, to give legal advice or counsel, perform for or furnish to another legal services, or, for or without a fee or any consideration, to prepare, directly or through another, for another person, firm, or corporation, any will or testamentary disposition or instrument of trust serving purposes similar to those of a will, or, for a fee or any consideration, to prepare for another person, firm, or corporation, any other legal document, **except as provided in subdivision 3.**

Subdivision. 3.   Permitted actions. The provisions of this section shall not prohibit:

(1) to (11) and (16) not listed here.

(12) **any authorized management agent** of an owner of rental property **used for residential purposes,** whether the management agent is a natural person, corporation, partnership, limited partnership, or any other business entity, **from commencing, maintaining, conducting, or defending in its own behalf any action in any court in this state to recover or retain possession of the property,** except that the provision of this clause does not authorize a person who is not a licensed attorney-at-law to conduct a jury trial or to appear before a district court or the Court of Appeals or Supreme Court pursuant to an appeal;

(13) **any person** from commencing, maintaining, conducting, or defending on behalf of the plaintiff or defendant any action **in any court of this state** pursuant to the provisions of section 504B.375 or sections 504B.185 and 504B.381 to 504B.471 or from commencing, maintaining, conducting, or defending on behalf of the plaintiff or defendant any action in any court of this state **for the recovery of rental property used for residential purposes** pursuant to the provisions of section 504B.285, subdivision 1, or 504B.301, except that the provision of this clause does not authorize a person who is not a licensed attorney-at-law to conduct a jury trial or to appear before a district court or the Court of Appeals or Supreme Court pursuant to an appeal, and provided that, except for a nonprofit corporation, a person who is not a licensed attorney-at-law shall

not charge or collect a separate fee for services rendered pursuant to this clause;

(14) the delivery of legal services by a specialized legal assistant in accordance with a specialty license issued by the Supreme Court before July 1, 1995;

(15) the **sole shareholder of a corporation from appearing on behalf of the corporation in court**; or

It is well settled law that the term "person" includes artificial beings, such as corporations and partnerships. Corporations are "persons" as that word is used in the first clause of the XIVth Amendment to the United States Constitution. Smyth vs. Ames, 169 U.S.466. It has been held that when the term person is used in a legislative act, natural persons will be intended unless something appears in the context to show that it applies to artificial persons. Blair v. Worley, 1 Scram. ILL. 178, Appeal of Fox, 112 Pa.337. But as a rule corporations will be considered persons within the Statutes unless the intention of the legislature is manifestly to exclude them. Scribbinling v. Bank. 5 Rand. Va. 132. See also: Blacks Law Dictionary.

It is clear from the intent of Rule 603 of the Housing Court Rules and Minn. Stat. 481.02 that the term "person" also includes artificial beings such as corporations and partnerships.

It is also clear from Minn. Stat. § 481.02 that agents may be corporations and that the sole shareholder of a corporation may appear for a corporation in court.

In light of the above caselaw and rules and statutes, in Hennepin County at least, agents may represent artificial persons such as corporations and limited liability companies in Housing Court proceedings involving residential property. In the event of any appeal to District Court or the Court of Appeals, a licensed attorney must then represent a corporation as required by Minn. Stat. § 481.02.   This is consistent with Nicollet Restoration, Inc. vs. Turnham 486 N.W. 2d 753 (Minn. 1992) which provided that a corporation must be represented by an attorney in an appeal from Conciliation Court to District Court for a trial de novo.

The issue on whether or not agents can represent artificial persons in Housing Court involving commercial property is a bit more clouded, since they are not authorized to do so under Minn. Stat. §481.02 but appear to be authorized under Rule 603 of Housing Court Rules.

At the present time, (2010) Hennepin County is the only County in the State that allows agents to represent corporations and limited liability companies in Housing Court. All the other counties in the State of Minnesota require corporations and limited liability companies to be represented by attorneys.

8. Audio Tape Evidence

The policy in the Fourth Judicial District is that the party intending to introduce a recorded statement (video and/or audio)[15] must, at the time the rules require disclosure of the statement, advise the opposing party of the format in which the statement is preserved (video, audio) and must, prior to the trial, timely prepare, serve and file a verbatim transcript of the recorded statement. The proponent of the recorded statement is responsible for its accurate transcription. Failure to comply with either requirement may result in exclusion of the recorded statement at trial.

9. Background Check on Property Managers

Minnesota Statutes 299C.68 requires Landlords to do Background checks on persons who are residential building managers for apartment buildings.

Before hiring a manager, an owner shall request the superintendent to conduct a background check. An owner may employ a manager after requesting a background check under this section before receipt of the background check report, provided that the owner complies with section 299C.69. An owner may request a background check for a currently employed manager under this section. By July 1, 1996, an owner shall request the superintendent to conduct a background check under this section for managers hired before July 1, 1995, who are currently employed.

If the superintendent's response indicates that the manager has been convicted of a background check crime defined in section 299C.67, subdivision 2, paragraph (a), the owner may not hire the manager or, if the manager was hired pending completion of the background check, shall terminate the manager's employment. Except as provided in paragraph (c), if an owner otherwise knows that a manager has been convicted of a background check crime defined in section 299C.67, subdivision 2, paragraph (a), the owner shall terminate the manager's employment.

A background check crime which would prohibit a Landlord from hiring or require the Landlord to terminate the manager would be as follows:

Background check crimes under 299C.67 are as follows (Note: Felony convictions required except for Stalking).

609.185 (first-degree murder);

609.19 (second-degree murder);

609.20 (first-degree manslaughter);

---

[15] This applies to, but is not limited to, all 911 calls, answering machine message, Scales tapes, child interviews, crime scene walk-throughs and depositions.

609.221 (first-degree assault);

609.222 (second-degree assault);

609.223 (third-degree assault);

609.25 (kidnapping);

609.342 (first-degree criminal sexual conduct);

609.343 (second-degree criminal sexual conduct);

609.344 (third-degree criminal sexual conduct);

609.345 (fourth-degree criminal sexual conduct);

609.561 (first-degree arson); or

609.749 (stalking); felony or **non felony**

 609.195 (third-degree murder);

609.205 (second-degree manslaughter);

609.21 (criminal vehicular homicide and injury);

609.2231 (fourth-degree assault);

609.224 (fifth-degree assault); 609.24 (simple robbery);

609.245 (aggravated robbery);

609.255 (false imprisonment);

609.52 (theft); 609.582, subdivision 1 or 2 (burglary);

609.713 (terroristic threats);

10. Bankruptcy

Section 362(22) states an automatic stay does not apply to the continuation of an eviction action by a landlord involving residential property in which the debtor resides under a lease and with respect to which the landlord has obtained, before the bankruptcy, a judgment for possession of the property.

The Bankruptcy Court in the case In Re Crawley, 117 B.R. 457, 23 Collier Bankr.Cas.2d 543, Bankr. L. Rep. P 73,574 (1990) held that: (1) mortgaged property was not possessed by estate, and thus second mortgagee's commencement of unlawful detainer action was not act to obtain possession of mortgaged premises "from the estate" in violation of automatic stay, and (2) debtor's post expiration possession of mortgaged property did not constitute "property of the estate," and thus commencement of unlawful detainer action was not act to obtain "property of the estate" in violation of automatic stay.

Automatic stay applies to all other situations. Need order lifting stay to proceed.

11. Bond on Appeal.

See Camber Hill Limited Partnership dba Camber Hill Townhomes vs. Edward Samuel and John Doe, et. al. (Court of Appeals A06-6, (unpublished 2006). This case states that the purpose of a supersedeas bond is to ensure that, pending the outcome of an appeal, the economic risk of the appeal is not borne by the party not in possession. Also see discussion under Appeals above.

12. Cash Rent Payments. Receipts.

A landlord receiving rent or other payments from a tenant in cash must provide a written receipt for payment immediately upon receipt if the payment is made in person, or within three business days if payment in cash is not made in person. (Minn. Stat. 504B.118) (2010 law effective August 1, 2010).

There is a rebuttable presumption under Minn. Stat. 504B.291 that the rent has been paid if the tenant produces a copy or copies of one or more money orders or produces one or more original receipt stubs evidencing the purchase of a money order, if it documents: (i) the total amount of the rent; (ii) includes a date or dates approximately corresponding with the date rent was due; and (iii) in the case of copies of money orders, are made payable to the landlord. This presumption is rebutted if the landlord produces a business record that shows that the tenant has not paid the rent. The landlord is not precluded from introducing other evidence that rebuts this presumption.

13. Certificate of Assumed Name.   Minn. Stat. 333.06

Landlords will often use assumed names for their leased property (e.g. Parkview Apartments). Often, Tenants will raise as a defense that Landlord's assumed name is not registered with the State of Minnesota. The rules regarding assumed names are as follows:

a. If any person files a civil action (including eviction actions) and is using an assumed name and has not filed a Certificate of Assumed name with the Secretary of State as required by Minn. Stat. 333.001 to 333.06, the defendant may plead such failure in abatement of the action; and all proceedings had in the action shall thereupon be stayed until the certificate provided for by sections 333.001 to 333.06 is duly filed, and if the defendant prevails in the action, the defendant shall also be entitled to tax $250 costs, in addition to such other statutory costs as may be allowed by law.

b. Minnesota Statutes 504B.285 states that a "person" entitled to possession may commence an action for eviction. Rule 603 of the Housing Court Rules states that an eviction action shall be brought in the name of the owner of the property or other "person" entitled to possession of the premises. Minnesota Statutes 504B.001 (definitions) states the following.

> Subd. 10. "Person" means a natural person, corporation, limited liability company, partnership, joint enterprise, or unincorporated association. A joint enterprise is a joint undertaking of different "persons" and is basically a partnership. Associations are generally organizations set up by Minnesota Statute that are usually organized as non profits. There are a number of different types of associations authorized by Minnesota Statutes (e.g. Teachers retirement fund association).

c. The above Statue and Court Rules make it clear that only a "person" may commence an action in Housing Court (or any civil action for that matter).

d. The question has been raised if a person may file an action under an "assumed name". Every rule and Statute regarding who may bring a civil action refers to a "person". No statute or rule allows persons to use assumed names when commencing civil actions. An assumed name such as "Roseville Apartments" is not a person. The Court needs to know what legal "person" is behind the name which fits into one of the above six listed under 504B.001 definitions.

e. Minnesota Statutes Chapter 333 states that no person shall carry on or conduct or transact a commercial business with an "assumed name" unless such person has filed a "Certificate of Assumed Name" in the Office of the Secretary of State. This statute further states that if any **person** commences a civil action and has been conducting a business with an assumed name and has not filed a Certificate of Assumed name with the Secretary of State, that the defendant may plead such failure as a defense to the action and Plaintiff could be penalized and his/her action dismissed due to this failure to be registered.

f. Nothing in Minn. Stat. 333 et sec authorizes anyone other than a person to commence a civil action and nothing in Minn. Stat. 333 et sec says that a person can commence a civil action under an assumed name.

g. Conclusion: only legal "persons" as defined above can commence an action in Minnesota Courts. The name of the "legal person" must be included in the pleadings and if the person is using an assumed name, the name of the legal person should be listed and state that they are doing business using an assumed name. Example: Stone, Inc. dba Rocky. The proper legal name or person is Stone, Inc. which is their corporate name, and their assumed name is Rocky.

14. Commercial leases.

Residential tenancies under Minnesota law are largely controlled by Minnesota Statutes 504B et sec. There are provisions of Minnesota Statutes 504B that apply to commercial leases, but many do not. Lockouts, Tenant Remedy Actions, Rent Escrow Actions, utility laws, Administrators, and provisions regarding personal property apply to residential properties only.

Commercial leases are enforced generally under the general principals of contract law. The United States Court of Appeals, Eighth Circuit, held in 1996 that:

> Under Minnesota Law, general principals of contract construction apply to commercial leases. Carlson Real Estate v. Soltan, 549 N.W.2d 376, 379 (Minn. App. 1996).

15. Condition Precedent.

This issue comes up in Housing Court cases because often both Landlord and Tenant have breached the lease. Tenant has breached the lease by not paying the rent and Landlord may have breached the lease by not making repairs as required by law. Often, the Court is asked to dismiss an eviction action due to a breach by the Landlord of a law or provision of the lease.

A condition precedent is an event that must occur before a party is required to perform a certain contractual duty. Carl Bolander & Sons, Inc. v. United Stockyards Corp., 298 Minn. 428, 433, 215 N.W.2d 473, 476 (1974). "[N]o particular code words [are] needed to form an express condition." Id. (citing 5 Samuel Williston, Williston on Contracts § 671 (3d ed. 1961)). In Aslakson v. Home Sav. Ass'n, 416 N.W.2d 786 (Minn.App.1987), the Minnesota Court of Appeals considered the effect of a contract requiring a party to establish credit as a condition precedent. The controversy involved a sales contract, which provided in relevant part, "This offer is contingent upon buyer being able to assume the loan." Id. at 787. The Court of Appeals concluded that this language created a condition precedent. Id. at 789. Because the purchaser was unable to demonstrate acceptable credit, the seller had no obligation to complete the sale. Id. at 790.

The Minnesota Supreme Court in *451 Corp. v. Pension Sys. for Policemen & Firemen,* 310 N.W.2d 922 (Minn.1981), reached the same conclusion based on a more complex set of facts. The owners of an office building had a short-term construction loan and sought long-term financing from a state pension fund. *Id. at 922.* The parties executed a contract, which stated that the loan was "subject to approval of the documents as to legality and form" by a state official. *Id. at 923.* On review of the contract, that state official found an illegal amortization and rejected the loan. *Id.* The Supreme Court concluded that, because the approval condition was not met, the pension fund had no obligation to supply the loan. *Id. at 924; see also Nat'l Union Fire Ins. v. Schwing America, Inc.,* 446 N.W.2d 410, 412 (Minn.App.1989) ("[A] breach of contract does not occur when a contract is conditioned on third-party approval and the approval is not received." (quoting *Aslaksan,* 416 N.W.2d at 789)). See: **Minnwest Bank Central v. Flagship Properties LLC** 689 N.W.2d 295 Minn.App.,2004. Dec 07, 2004 (Approx. 13 pages).

Where the right to demand the performance of a certain act depends on the execution by the promisee of a **condition precedent** or prior act, it is clear that the readiness and offer of the latter to fulfill the **condition**, and the hindrance of its performance by the promisor, are in law equivalent to the completion of the **condition precedent**, and will render the promisor liable upon his contract. Graves v. Legg, 9 Exch. 709; *Morton v. Lamb,* 7 Term, 125; 2 Wms. Saund. 352 *b*; 2 Smith, Lead. Cas. 13. **Jones v. U.S.** 96 U.S. 24   Oct Term 1877 (Approx. 6 pages).

Normally, in order to create a **condition precedent**, an agreement must use a term such as "on condition that," "if," "provided that," or some similar conditional phrase. McMahon, 108 S.W.3d at 484. While there is no requirement that such phrases be utilized, their absence is probative of the parties' intention that a promise be made, rather than a condition imposed. Cal-Tex, 989 S.W.2d at 809.   Because of the harshness in operation, **conditions precedent** are not favored in law, and courts will not construe a contract provision as a **condition precedent** unless they are compelled to do so by language that may be construed in no other way. Id.

Whether to dismiss a case based on a condition precedent will be up to the discretion of the Judge.[16] Look to see whether or not the alleged breach by the Landlord was prior to the alleged breach by the Tenant. Also, look to see if the breach is a statutory breach or not. Fact situations where proper to dismiss based on this theory are as follows:

> i)   Failure to give a copy of the lease to Tenant as required by Minn. Stat. 504B.115.

---

[16] (I am not including improper service or process or improper notice issues in this category. These could of course be immediately dismissed**).**

ii) Failure of Landlord to properly disclose to Tenant information required in Minn. Stat. 504B.181. (must be done 30 days prior to commencing action and address must NOT be a P.O. Box).

iii) Partial payment of rent and no written agreement required by Minn. Stat. 504B.291.

There are other defenses raised where the Defendants will ask for immediate dismissal where Court should not do so without a hearing so that you can make findings. Tenants will often ask the Court to dismiss an eviction action involving Section 8 vouchers because Landlord has not served the Housing Authority with a copy of the Summons and Complaint.

In Section 8 cases there are three parties involved: Landlord, Tenant, and the Housing Authority. The Housing Authority will rarely be a party to the action. However, in all Section 8 cases the Landlord has a contract with the Housing Authority which states that a Tenancy Addendum (Part C) must be attached to the lease which requires Landlord to serve a copy of the Eviction action on the Housing Authority at the same time the eviction action is served on Tenant. The Tenant has a right to enforce this provision. If the Housing Authority is not served, Landlord is in violation of the lease requirement that the Housing Authority be served. The question is then raised should the Court dismiss based on this breach, proceed with action and address this breach at trial, or should the Court require service or joinder as allowed by Rule 19 of the Rules of Civil Procedure?[17] Often the Tenant will admit they are in breach of the lease also by owing rent so you have a situation where both parties are in breach. What is the right thing to do?

A rule in the law of contracts is that a party cannot raise to its advantage a breach of contract against another party when it has first breached the contract itself. MTS vs. Taiga 365 N.W.2d 321 (Minn. App. 1985) Cheezem Development Corp. v. Intracoastal Sales and Service, Inc., 336 So.2d. 1210, 1212 (Fla.Ct.App.1976); Yonan v. Oak Park Federal Savings and Loan Association, 326 N.E.2d 773, 781 (Ill.App.1975); Robinhorne Construction Corp. v. Snyder, 251 N.E.2d 641, 645-46 (Ill.App.1969), aff'd, 265 N.E.2d 670 (Ill.1970). Cf. Verran v. Blacklock, 60 Mich.App. 763, 231 N.W.2d 544, 547 (1975);

---

[17] The Code of Federal Regulations require the Landlord to serve notice on the Housing Authority of any eviction action but do not require this notice to be at the time of the commencement of the action. Prior to 1995, 24 C.F.R. §§ 882.215(c)(1) and 887.213(c) provided that the owner must notify the housing authority in writing at the same time that the owner gives notice to the tenant under state or local law. In 1995 this regulation was changed to simply state: "The owner must give the HA [housing authority] a copy of any owner eviction notice to the tenant." 24 C.F.R. § 982.310(e)(2)(ii), 60 Fed. Reg. at 34,705. The time requirement that it be served at the same time was eliminated.

Odysseys Unlimited, Inc. v. Astral Travel Service, 77 Misc.2d 502, 354 N.Y.S.2d 88, 91 (Sup.Ct.1974). In the Taiga case the rule was applied because in that case Plaintiff's initial breach was a cause of the alleged breach by defendant. Usually in these Landlord Tenant relationships, the failure by the Landlord to notify HUD in violation of the lease is not a "first breach" and usually has no relationship to the breach of tenant which is either breach of lease or non payment of rent. Probably the best course of action is to look at the facts on a case by case basis to decide what is fair and equitable under the circumstances.

There are certainly "condition Precedents" in Section 8 HUD leases where Landlord's are required to do certain things, including giving Tenant written notices, etc. which must be done prior to commencement of the eviction action. See case Hoglund-Hall v. Kleinschmidt, 381 N.W.2d 889 (Minn. App. 1986) in which the court dismissed the action because Landlord did not comply with federal housing regulations regarding pre eviction notice.

16. Contract for Deed Cancellation

Plaintiffs are entitled to possession of property pursuant to Minn. Stat. 504B.285 which provides under Subdivision 1 that The person entitled to the premises may recover possession by eviction when any person holds over real property:

after termination of contract to convey the property, provided that if the person holding the real property after the expiration of the time for redemption or termination is a tenant, the person has received:

(A) at least two month's written notice to vacate no sooner than one month after the expiration of the time for redemption or termination, provided that the tenant pays the rent and abides by all terms of the lease; or

(B) at least two month's written notice to vacate no later than the date of the expiration of the time for redemption or termination, which notice shall also state that the sender will hold the tenant harmless for breaching the lease by vacating the premises if the mortgage is redeemed or the contract is reinstated;

17. Costs

HNA Properties vs. Monica Moore, A13-0870 (Minn. App. 2014) Published Case.

According to the plain language of Minn. Stat. § 549.02, subd. 1 (2012), a defendant is entitled to $200 in costs upon dismissal of a case.

A party who obtains a dismissal for procedural reasons is not a prevailing party

Minn. Stat. § 563.01, subd. 10 (2012), does not apply when a defendant is awarded statutory costs as a result of the district court's dismissal of a case

The district court interpreted the statute's language differently. Instead of applying the clause "on the merits" to only the last alternative listed in the statute, the district court applied it to each of the three alternatives. As a result, the district court found that Moore was not entitled to costs because there was no adjudication on the merits. But the plain language of the statute establishes that each of the three alternatives is distinct from the others. And we note that it is impossible to apply "on the merits" to all of the alternatives. For example, "discontinuance" is defined as "[t]he termination of a lawsuit by the plaintiff" and "a voluntary dismissal or nonsuit." *Black's Law Dictionary* 532 (9th ed. 2009). "On the merits" is defined as "delivered after the court has heard and evaluated the evidence and the parties' substantive arguments." *Black's Law Dictionary* 1199 (9th ed. 2009). Thus, discontinuance "on the merits" is impossible.

The statute states that "costs shall be allowed as follows," and then separately lists the "plaintiff," the "defendant," and "the prevailing party." Minn. Stat. § 549.02, subd. 1. The fact that the statute lists three separate provisions indicates that they should be considered separately. If the legislature intended the $5.50 in costs to apply to the party who is allowed statutory costs, it could have included those costs under the "plaintiff" and "defendant" provisions of the statute. However, the legislature separately provided that $5.50 in costs must be allowed to "the prevailing party." The plain language of the statute indicates that the district court must allow the statutory $5.50 in costs to the prevailing party and only the prevailing party, if there is one, regardless of which party is allowed costs under the other provisions of the statute.

The prevailing party in any action is one in whose favor the decision or verdict is rendered and judgment entered." *Borchert v. Maloney*, 581 N.W.2d 838, 840 (Minn. 1998) (quotation omitted). The district court has "discretion to determine which party, if any, qualifies as a prevailing party." *Benigni v. Cnty. of St. Louis*, 585 N.W.2d 51, 54-55 (Minn. 1998). This court reviews an award of costs for an abuse of discretion. *Id.* at 54.

However, we conclude that a prevailing party must be more than "successful to some degree," and instead must "prevail[] on the merits in the underlying action." *Borchert*, 581 N.W.2d at 8

840; *see Elsenpeter v. St. Michael Mall, Inc.*, 794 N.W.2d 667, 673 (Minn. App. 2011) ("A plaintiff 'must receive at least some relief on the merits of his claim before he can be said to prevail.'" (quoting *Hewitt v. Helms*, 482 U.S. 755, 760, 107 S. Ct. 2672, 2675 (1987))).

"Costs and disbursements, when given as here by statute, are an incident to a recovery or a successful defense." *State v. Kylamen*, 178 Minn. 164, 173, 226 N.W.2d 709, 710 (1929). The statutory costs that Moore is entitled to receive are not a recovery of money upon settlement or judgment because the statutory costs are merely incidental to the dismissal, which is not a settlement or judgment. Therefore, Minn. Stat. § 563.01, subd. 10, does not apply in this case and the district court erred by finding that any costs due to Moore would have to be paid directly to the court administrator.

18. Damage (Security) Deposit.

Minn. Stat. 504B.178 deals with issues regarding damage or security deposits. In the 2010 legislative session, the penalty to Landlord for bad faith retention of the security deposits was increased to $500.00.

19. Disability in Housing (Reasonable Accommodation).

If a Tenant is disabled within the MHRA definition, they are entitled to reasonable accommodation of their disabilities with respect to access to residential rental premises under Minn.Stat.Sec.363A.10. To be disabled means you must be significantly restricted in your ability due to the physical impairment. A violation of Landlord's responsibility could be a condition precedent that could warrant dismissal of the eviction action.

See, e.g., Snow v. Ridgeview Medical Center, 128 F.3d 1201, 1206 *Shapiro v. Cadman Towers, Inc.*,51 F.3d 328, 332-333 (2d Cir. 1995), *Jankowski Lee & Associates v. Cisneros*, 91 F.3d 891, 895 (7th Cir1996).

20. Discrimination in Housing

Owners and managing agents who "refuse to sell, rent, or lease or otherwise deny to or withhold from any person . . . any real property because of . . . status with regard to public assistance" commit an unlawful discriminatory act under the MHRA. Minn. Stat. § 363A.09, subd. 1(1). "„Status with regard to public assistance" means the condition of being a . . . tenant receiving federal, state, or local subsidies, including rental assistance or rent supplements." Minn. Stat. § 363A.03, subd. 47 (2008). A plaintiff may show discrimination under the MHRA by using the McDonnell-Douglas burden-shifting framework. Goins v. West Group, 635 N.W.2d 717, 722-23, 724 n.3 (Minn. 2001); see McDonnell Douglas Corp. v. Green, 411 U.S. 792, 802-04, 93 S. Ct. 1817, 1824-25 (1973) (setting out framework).   A plaintiff may also establish discrimination through direct evidence. Goins, 635 N.W.2d at 722-23.

Recent Minnesota Court of Appeals case held that a decision by a property owner to end participation in a Section 8 housing choice voucher program and to consequently stop renting to a Section 8 tenant does NOT constitute discrimination based on a Tenant's status with regard to public assistance under Minn. Stat. section 363A.09 subd. 1 (2008). See Edwards v. Hopkins Plaza Limited Partnership (Minn. Ct. App 2010 file No. A09-1616).

21. Domestic Abuse

A tenant to a residential lease (private market with no federal HUD subsidy involved) who is a victim of domestic abuse and fears imminent domestic abuse against the tenant or the tenant's minor children if the tenant or the tenant's minor children remain in the leased premises may terminate a lease agreement without penalty or liability as provided in Minnesota Stat. 504B.206. The tenant must provide advance written notice to the landlord stating that:

(1) The tenant fears imminent domestic abuse from a person named in an order for protection or no contact order[18];

(2) The tenant needs to terminate the tenancy; and

(3) The specific date the tenancy will terminate.

The written notice must be delivered before the termination of the tenancy by mail, fax, or in person, and be accompanied by the order for protection or no contact order.

A tenant terminating a lease under this law is responsible for the rent payment for the full month in which the tenancy terminates and an additional amount equal to one month's rent. The tenant is relieved of any other contractual obligation for payment of rent or any other charges for the remaining term of the lease, except as provided in this section. This section does not affect a tenant's liability for delinquent, unpaid rent or other amounts owed to the landlord.

A tenant in a lease in which HUD is involved such as Section 8 or public subsidized leases would have rights under the Federal Violence against Women Act (VAWA).   Leases in which VAWA would apply include public housing programs, Section 8 vouchers, Project based Section 8, Section 202 Elderly housing, Housing for persons with Aids, Section 811 housing for people with disabilities and housing funded with HOME funds.

VAWA provides protection for victims of domestic abuse, including protection from eviction for victims of domestic abuse, and right to terminate lease and have housing voucher transfer to other housing, among other protections.

22. Ejectment.

An eviction is "a summary court proceeding to remove a tenant or occupant from or otherwise recover possession of real property by the process of law set out in [chapter 504B]." Minn.Stat. §§ 504B.001, subd. 4 (2002). **Ejectment** is an action for possession of real estate in which the plaintiff must show a present or immediate right of possession and a legal estate in the property sought to be recovered.   *Levine v. Twin City Red Barn No. 2, Inc., 296 Minn. 260, 263, 207 N.W.2d 739, 741 (1973).*

Basically, if there is no Landlord Tenant relationship, and you claim an ownership interest in the property, you need to bring an action for ejectment.

23. Emergency Assistance

---

[18] For purposes of this section, an order for protection means an order issued under chapter 518B. A no contact order means a no contact order currently in effect, issued under section 629.75 or chapter 609.

Emergency Assistance is available to help Tenants pay rent from the Human Services and Public Health Department. Here is some basic information about Emergency Assistance as of December, 2009.

      a. Assistance for single persons was phased out on October 31, 2009.

      b. Assistance for families currently has inflated because of federal stimulus money. Persons may ask for assistance up to twice a year, the prior rule was only once a year. Families means you must have a minor child, 18 years of age and younger, or be pregnant.

      c. Emergency assistance income limits are 200% of federal poverty guidelines. May have minor or child 18 years old if in high school.

      d. Emergency assistance will pay the following: 1) security deposit, 2) up to two months' rent, 3) court costs, and 4) unpaid utilities up to $10,000.00.

      e. Tenants who have a court order are given priority and a decision will be paid within a week's time.

      f. Tenants must have the following information to get emergency assistance:
          i) Photo ID
          ii) Income Verification
          iii) Verification of relationship to child (birth certificate, etc.). Child must be a U.S. citizen.
          iv) Copy of lease or some other verification of rent due.
          v) Copy of court order allowing redemption.
          vi) Verification from Landlord (usually by phone). Need phone number.

      g. If Tenant is getting public assistance already they will probably not need all of the above verification information.

24. Equity- Inherent Authority

Equity functions as a supplement to the rest of the law where its remedies are inadequate to do complete justice. Swogger v. Taylor, 243 Minn. 458; 68 N.W.2d 376 (Minn. 1955). Equity characteristically possesses the flexibility and expansiveness to invent new remedies or modify old ones to meet the requirements of every case and to satisfy the needs of a progressive social condition. Beliveau v. Beliveau 217 Minn. 235, 14 N.W.2d 360 (Minn. 1944).

Generally, equity will not grant relief where there is an adequate remedy at law. Generally, the decision to grant equitable relief is within the sound discretion of the district court and its decision regarding such relief will not be reversed absent an abuse of that discretion. Nadeau v. County of Ramsey, 277 N.W.2d 520, 524 (Minn.1979) Classen v. City of Lauderdale, 681 N.W.2d 722, (Minn. App. 2004).

Generally, the decision to grant equitable relief is within the sound discretion of the district court and its decision regarding such relief will not be reversed absent an abuse of that discretion. Nadeau v. County of Ramsey, 277 N.W.2d 520, 524 (Minn.1979). In an action to determine adverse property claims, a district court has jurisdiction to determine any interests or issues that are fairly covered by the pleadings and evidence presented. See Neill v. Hake, 254 Minn. 110, 116-17, 93 N.W.2d 821, 827 (1958) (holding that court had jurisdiction to reform deeds in action to quiet title, even though exact relief not requested in pleadings). Thus, while respondents may not specifically have requested relief in the form of a prescriptive easement, we will assume for the purposes of this appeal that the district court had jurisdiction to grant such relief in this action to quiet title or for adverse possession.

Nevertheless, a district court cannot sua sponte exercise its inherent authority to grant equitable relief in a manner that prejudices the opposing party by failing to give it an opportunity to present evidence to oppose the relief ultimately given. See Del Hayes & Sons, Inc. v. Mitchell, 304 Minn. 275, 280, 230 N.W.2d 588, 592 (1975) (stating court has inherent power to sua sponte summarily dispose of case in which no genuine issue of material fact exists). In addition, a district court's decision to grant equitable relief is not unlimited and must be supported by the facts and law. See Lindell v. Lindell, 150 Minn. 295, 299, 185 N.W. 929, 930 (1921) (stating that court "is invested with no arbitrary discretion; that is, a judge may not impose conditions [or grant relief] which in his individual opinion would work substantial justice between the parties," without regard to precedents and established principles).

25. Expungement.

Motions to expunge Housing Court files are authorized under Minn. Stat. 484.014. Expungement motions should be in writing and signed by the Tenant.19   Minn. Stat. 484.014 does not say anything about the notice period for expungement motions. Housing Court in Hennepin County requires that ten days written notice mailed to the other party shall be given for expungement motions. This requirement is based on Rule 6.04 of the Minnesota Rules of Civil Procedure which requires that written motions must be served no later than 5 days before the time specified for the hearing, unless a different period is fixed by the rules or by order of the court. Since weekend days do not count in the computation of the time under Rule 6.01 the time for service was extended to seven days. Adding three days for service by mail makes the total time ten days and Housing Court has determined that at a minimum, there should be at least ten days written notice of expungement motions when served by mail.

The issue in expungement motions is whether Landlord's case was sufficiently without basis in fact or law, which may include lack of jurisdiction over the case. The court must find that expungement is clearly in the interests of justice and those interests are not outweighed by the public's interest in knowing about the record.

---

[19] Rule 7.02 of Rules of Civil procedure says a motion, unless made during the hearing or trial, shall be in writing.

Mandatory Expungment: Minn. Stat. 484.014 states that a court **shall** order expungement of an eviction case commenced solely on the grounds provided in section 504B.285, subdivision 1, clause (1), (foreclosures) if the court finds that the defendant occupied real property that was subject to contract for deed cancellation or mortgage foreclosure and: (1) the time for contract cancellation or foreclosure redemption has expired and the defendant vacated the property prior to commencement of the eviction action; or (2) the defendant was a tenant during the contract cancellation or foreclosure redemption period and did not receive a notice under section 504B.285, subdivision 1a, 1b or 1c, , to vacate on a date prior to commencement of the eviction case.

26. Filing of Affidavits.

Occasionally issues will arise where Tenants will ask the court to dismiss the eviction case due to improper or untimely filing of Affidavits of Service.

The Housing Court Rules has language regarding the filing of Affidavits which state as follows:

Rule 605. Return of Summons

*All summons shall be served in the manner required by Minnesota Statutes, Chapter 504B, **and the affidavit of service shall be filed with the court by 3:00 o'clock p.m. 3 business days prior to the hearing** or the matter may be stricken. The affidavit must contain the printed or typed name of the person who served the summons.*

Rule 606. Filing of Affidavits

Upon return of the sheriff or other process server indicating that the defendant cannot be found in the county and, in the case of a nonresidential premises, where no person actually occupies the premises described in the complaint, or, in the case the premises described in the complaint is residential, service has been attempted at least twice on different days, with at least one of the attempts having been made between the hours of 6:00 and 10:00 p.m., the plaintiff or plaintiff's lawyer shall:

>*(1) file an affidavit stating that the defendant cannot be found or on belief that the defendant is not in the state, and*

>*(2) file an affidavit stating that a copy of the summons and complaint has been mailed to the defendant at the defendant's last known address or that such an address is unknown to the plaintiff.*

Service of the summons may be made upon the defendant by posting the summons in a conspicuous place on the premises for not less than one week. A separate affidavit shall be filed stating that the summons has been posted and the date and location of the posting. (Amended effective January 1, 1998.)

Minn. Stat. 504B.331 provides how Housing Court Eviction actions may be commenced and in this statute there is language about the filing of affidavits which states as follows:

(d) Where the defendant cannot be found in the county, service of the summons may be made upon the defendant by posting the summons in a conspicuous place on the property for not less than one week if:

> *(1) the property described in the complaint is:*
>
> > *(i) nonresidential and no person actually occupies the property; or*
> >
> > *(ii) residential and service has been attempted at least twice on different days, with at least one of the attempts having been made between the hours of 6:00 p.m. and 10:00 p.m.; and*
>
> *(2) the plaintiff or the plaintiff's attorney has signed and filed with the court an affidavit stating that:*
>
> > *(i) the defendant cannot be found, or that the plaintiff or the plaintiff's attorney believes that the defendant is not in the state; and*
> >
> > *(ii) a copy of the summons has been mailed to the defendant at the defendant's last known address if any is known to the plaintiff.*

Tenants will on occasion argue that this statute must be interpreted so that in order to post the Summons, the Landlord must make at least three trips to the courthouse and three trips to the leased property as follows:

> **Trip One**: Landlord comes to courthouse to pay filing fee and receive Summons and Complaint. Landlord then goes out to leased property twice and makes two attempts on different days to serve Tenant. Landlord mails Summons to Tenant.
>
> **Trip Two**: Landlord makes second trip to courthouse to file Affidavit of Not Found and Affidavit of Mailing. Landlord then goes back out to leased property for the third time to post.
>
> **Trip Three**: Landlord makes third trip to courthouse to file Affidavit of Posting and must also file the Affidavit of Plaintiff.

Landlords will argue that the service Statute (Minn. Stat. 504B.331) does not require Landlord to make three trips to courthouse. Landlord does not dispute that the Affidavits of service must be filed but argues that the statute does not specifically require some affidavits to be filed prior to posting. Landlords will argue that if the interpretation of the statute required three trips to the courthouse that this would effectively make it very difficult if not impossible to have the sheriff serve eviction summons. Landlords would not have enough time to go to the courthouse, then to the Sheriff for service, then back to the Sheriff to get the Affidavit of Not Found, then back to the Courthouse, then back to the Sheriff to have the Sheriff Post, then back to the Sheriff again to get the Affidavit of Posting, and then back to the Courthouse again.

There have been prior District Court opinions in Hennepin County which have held that the Affidavit of Not Found must actually be "filed" before the posting. Some of these decisions refer to the word "has" to decide this means that the filing must actually occur prior to the posting.

I have been told by Landlord Attorneys that other Counties do not require that the actual filing of the Affidavits of Not Found and Mailing must be done prior to the posting.

Rule 605 clearly requires that the "affidavit of service" be filed three business days prior to the hearing **or the matter "may" be stricken**.

The other rule of Civil Procedure related to filing is **Rule 5**. Rule 5 states that when there is a failure to comply with the requirements of this rule, the court in which the action is pending may make such orders as are just, including but not limited to, an order striking pleadings or parts thereof, staying further proceedings until compliance is complete, or dismissing the action, proceeding, or any part thereof.

There are many good reasons to require timely filing of affidavits and other pleadings, but the penalty for untimely filing is generally not dismissal of an action. Most of the time, the court will address the possible prejudice and make orders to ensure that the other party is not put at a disadvantage due to late filing. The dismissal of an action is clearly an option, but is generally NOT required.

In an unpublished case titled <u>Central Internal Medicine Association P.A. v. Chilgren</u>, No. C2-00-36, 2000 WL 987858 (Minn. Ct. App, July 18, 2000) the Court of Appeals made the following statement:

> *In interpreting the section of the unlawful-detainer statutes governing the contents of the complaint and summons, this court recently concluded that substantial compliance may be applied to the statutory requirement that the summons state "that the original [complaint] has been filed."* **Times Square Shopping Ctr., LLP v. Tobacco City, Inc.,** *585 N.W.2d 791, 792 (Minn. App. 1998) (interpreting Minn. Stat. § 566.05(a) (Supp. 1997),*

predecessor to Minn. Stat. § 504B.321, subd. 1(e) (Supp. 1999)), **review denied** (Minn. Jan. 21, 1999). *This court recognized in* **Times Square** *that although the eviction summons did not state that the original complaint had been filed, as the statute required, it did state that appellant was to appear at a certain date, time, and place.* **Id.** *The eviction summons substantially complied with Minn. Stat. § 566.05(a) because the court date could not have been scheduled unless the complaint was filed and because appellant was personally served with a copy of the summons and complaint, which contained an initialed date stamp and a handwritten case number.* **Id.**

As this court recognized in **Times Square**, *"A summons is 'a mere notice' that 'must substantially comply with the requirements of the rules' governing the service and form of process."* **Id.** *(quoting* **Tharp v. Tharp**, *228 Minn. 23, 24, 36 N.W.2d 1, 2 (1949) and* **Haas v. Brandvold**, *418 N.W.2d 511, 513 (Minn. App. 1988)).*[2] *Similar to the challenge to the form of the summons in* **Times Square**, *the Chilgrens are objecting only to the form of the affidavit sent to the district court and not to the service of the summons itself. Because it is undisputed that the process server posted the summons and mailed a copy to the Chilgrens' last known address, "the function of the eviction notice was not negated by the minor technical error."* **Id.** *We conclude the district court had subject matter jurisdiction over this unlawful-detainer action.*

The Court of Appeals in the Times Square case stated as follows:

A summons is "a mere notice" that "must substantially comply with the requirements of the rules" governing the service and form of process. **Tharp v. Tharp**, *228 Minn. 23, 24, 36 N.W.2d 1, 2 (1949);* **Haas v. Brandvold**, *418 N.W.2d 511, 513 (Minn. App. 1988). It is fundamental that cases should be decided on the merits rather than on technicalities, and where the intended recipient receives actual notice of the action, the rules governing such service should be liberally construed * * *.* **Pederson v. Clarkson Lindley Trust**, *519 N.W.2d 234, 235 (Minn. App. 1994).*

In the Times Square case, Defendants argued that the eviction case should be dismissed because the eviction summons (a standard form) did not state that the original complaint had been filed. Defendants argued that the statute governing eviction actions required the Summons to state that it had been filed.

In the Times Square case, the Court of Appeals focused more on the actual notice and the merits, rather than the technicalities of the filing requirement.

Conclusion: Courts have discretion and right to strike or dismiss a case or assess a penalty if a party improperly files a pleading but this court is NOT required to do so. Issues the court would address are prejudice to the other side, inconvenience on the court and its staff to have time to make sure everything is properly filed and in the file prior to the hearing, and compliance with the rules and statutes. There is no question that District Court Judges have exercised their discretion to dismiss cases where pleadings and affidavits were not filed correctly, but that does not mean Judges are required to do that.

27. Foreclosure Reconveyance- 90 day Automatic Stay

Minnesota Statute § 325N.18, subd 6 states that at a court hearing an eviction action against a foreclosed homeowner must issue an automatic stay, without imposition of a bond, if defendant makes a prima facie showing that the defendant:

a. asserts a defense under section 504B.121 that the property that is the subject of the eviction action is also the subject of a foreclosure reconveyance in violation of sections 325N.10 - 325N.17;

b. owned the foreclosed residence;

c. conveyed title to the foreclosed residence to a third party upon a promise that the defendant would be allowed to occupy the foreclosed residence in which the **foreclosure purchaser or a person acting in participation with the foreclosure purchaser** has an interest and that the foreclosed residence or other real property would be the subject of a foreclosed reconveyance; and

d. since the conveyance, has continuously occupied the foreclosed residence **in which the foreclosure purchaser or a person acting in participation with the foreclosure purchaser has an interest.**

The automatic stay expires upon the later of:

(a) the failure of the foreclosed homeowner to commence an action in a court of competent jurisdiction in connection with a foreclosed reconveyance transaction within **90 days** after the issuance of the stay; or

(b) the issuance of an order lifting the stay by a court hearing claims related to the foreclosure reconveyance.

If, after the expiration of the stay or an order lifting the stay, a court finds that the defendant's claim or defense was asserted in bad faith and wholly without merit, the court may impose a sanction against the defendant of $500 plus reasonable attorney fees.

Issues that present themselves in these situations are factual situations where the foreclosure purchaser or a person who acted in participation with the foreclosure purchaser no longer has an interest in the property. The language under Minn. Stat. 325N subd. 6a. does appear to say that the 90 day stay only applies if the *the foreclosure purchaser or a person acting in participation with the foreclosure purchaser* still has an interest in the property at the time of the eviction.

Occasionally, you may have a case where the foreclosure purchaser transferred the property to a third party who had nothing to do with the foreclosure reconveyance. The question raised will be does the 90 day automatic stay still apply.

Minn. Stat. 325N.10 Subd. 4 defines **Foreclosure purchaser as** a person that has acted as the acquirer in a foreclosure reconveyance. Foreclosure purchaser also includes a person that has acted in joint venture or joint enterprise with one or more acquirers in a foreclosure reconveyance. A foreclosure purchaser does not include: (i) a natural person who is not in the business of foreclosure purchasing and has a prior personal relationship with the foreclosed homeowner, or (ii) a federal or state chartered bank, savings bank, thrift, or credit union.

Minn. Stat. 325N.10 Subd. 5 defines "Resale" as a bona fide market sale of the property subject to the foreclosure reconveyance by the foreclosure purchaser to an unaffiliated third party.

The issue then, when a unaffiliated third party is involved in the eviction case is whether or not the third party purchased the property in a "bona fide" purchase. There is common law regarding what is bona fide or not and this is a fact based decision for the court to make. Generally, I will apply the 90 day stay to these fact situations unless I find that there was actually a "bona fide" transfer to an unaffiliated third party.

28. Group Residential Housing Facility

"Group residential housing" means a group living situation that provides at a minimum room and board to unrelated persons who meet the eligibility requirements of section 256I.04. This definition includes foster care settings for a single adult. To receive payment for a group residence rate, the residence must meet the requirements under section 256I.04, subdivision 2a. Generally, in order to be eligible, a person must be aged, blind, disabled and have low or no income. Most persons who live in these facilities have an illness or incapacity which prevents the person from living independently in the community; and the individual's illness or incapacity requires the services which are available in the group residence. Most persons who live in these facilities received rental assistance from the County or State. Secure crisis shelters for battered women and their children designated by the Minnesota Department of Corrections are not group residences under this chapter.

The question for the court is whether or not persons who live at these Group residential housing facilities are residential tenants as defined in Minn. Stat. 504B.001 subd. 12. If these residents are considered residential Tenants then the protections of Minn. Stat. 504B.375 would apply to them and it would be unlawful for the Group Home's to lock remove the residents from the Group Home without seeking an eviction order.

Minn. Stat. 504B.001 subd. 11 and 12 define Residential buildings and Residential Tenants as follows:

Subd. 11. **Residential building.** "Residential building" means:

(1) a building used in whole or in part as a dwelling, including single-family homes, multiple-family units such as apartments, and structures containing both dwelling units and units used for nondwelling purposes, and includes a manufactured home park; or

(2) an unoccupied building which was previously used in whole or in part as a dwelling and which constitutes a nuisance under section 561.01.

Subd. 12. **Residential tenant.** "Residential tenant" means a person who is occupying a dwelling in a residential building under a lease or contract, whether oral or written, that requires the payment of money or exchange of services, all other regular occupants of that dwelling unit, or a resident of a manufactured home park.

My interpretation of Minn. Stat. 504B and Minn. Stat. 256I shows that there is nothing in Minn. Stat. 256I that states that Tenants who reside in Group Residential Facilities are not Tenants as defined in Minn. Stat. 504B.001. Most Group homes try to work with their residents and try to help them relocate if they decide to evict them for non compliance with their rules and regulations. However, if they cannot work something out with the resident, then it is my belief that these residential Tenants are entitled to the protections of Minn. Stat. 504B. The Group Homes may certainly evict residents if they have violated terms of their Tenancy, *(eviction actions are summary in nature and a hearing can be scheduled in the expedited process in only 5 days)* but these Group Homes may not simply lock him residents without some due process. If Plaintiff commits any criminal acts of violence or assault, Defendant can call the police to seek more immediate relief.

This is an area of the law that the legislature should clarify. However, short of statutory exemption, it is my belief that where there is a dispute, these residential Group home Tenants have the right to due process before they can be removed from these homes.

29. Guardian.

Where Defendant's competence is in question the Court shall appoint a Guardian Ad Litem on behalf of Defendant pursuant to Rule 17.02 of the Minnesota Rules of Civil Procedure. When a Guardian is appointed, the Court should clarify what authority the Guardian has. Here are sample provisions for a Guardian order:

a. The Guardian ad Litem shall be notified of all proceedings. Sanctions may be available upon motion of the Guardian ad Litem should there be deliberate or negligent omission of notice to the Guardian ad Litem.

b. The Guardian ad Litem may initiate and respond to motions, conduct discovery, call and cross-examine witnesses, make oral or written arguments or reports, and appeal on behalf of the Defendant.

c. The Guardian ad Litem shall have the authority to request copies of all pleadings previously submitted by the parties.

d. That if the parties come to an agreement, mediated or otherwise, regarding substantive issues surrounding this matter, the Guardian ad Litem shall be required to review and sign the agreement before it is presented to the court officer for approval.

30. Hazardous Buildings.

Pursuant to Minn. Stat. §463.19 the District Court, upon the presentation of such evidence as it may require, has the authority to affirm or modify the Order for the Correction of Hazardous Conditions and the Abatement of Public Nuisances and enter judgment accordingly, fixing a time after which the governing body may proceed with the enforcement of the order. This allows a City to tear down or remove a building that the City considers hazardous. The key issue in these cases is to make sure all parties with an interest in the property were given proper notice as required by Minn. Stat. §463.17.

31. Hotel Guest vs. Tenant.

Sometimes there is a question as to whether or not a Defendant is a "Guest" at a Hotel or a Tenant. If Plaintiff is a "Guest" then his eviction would be governed by **Minn. Stat. 327.73**. If Plaintiff is a Tenant, then his eviction would be governed by Landlord Tenant law under Minn. Stat. Chapter 504B.

There are several terms which are important for the court to consider in this matter. Under Minn. Stat.327.70, which governs Hotels, the following definitions apply:

> *Subd. 2.* ***Guest.*** *"Guest" means a person who is registered at a hotel and to whom a bedroom is assigned. The term "guest" includes members of the guest's family who accompany the guest.*

> *Subd. 3.* ***Hotel.*** *"Hotel" means a hotel, motel, resort, boarding house, bed and breakfast, furnished apartment house or other building, which is kept, used or advertised as, or held out to the public to be, a place where sleeping or housekeeping accommodations are supplied for pay to guests for* ***transient occupancy.***

> *Subd. 5.* ***Transient occupancy.*** *"Transient occupancy" means occupancy when it is the intention of the parties that the occupancy will be temporary. There is a rebuttable presumption that, if the unit occupied is the sole residence of the guest, the occupancy is not transient. There is a rebuttable presumption that, if the unit occupied is not the sole residence*
> *of the guest, the occupancy is transient.*

Under Minn. Stat. 327.73, a Hotel Innkeeper may remove or cause to be removed a "Guest or other person" who:

(1) refuses or is unable to pay for accommodations or services;

(2) while on the premises of the hotel acts in an obviously intoxicated or disorderly manner, destroys or threatens to destroy hotel property, or causes or threatens to cause a disturbance;

(3) the innkeeper reasonably believes is using the premises for the unlawful possession or use of controlled substances by the person in violation of chapter 152, or using the premises for the consumption of alcohol by a person under the age of 21 years in violation of section 340A.503;

(4) the innkeeper reasonably believes has brought property into the hotel that may be dangerous to other persons, such as firearms or explosives;

(5) violates any federal, state, or local laws, ordinances, or rules relating to the hotel; or

(6) violates a rule of the hotel that is clearly and conspicuously posted at or near the front desk and on the inside of the entrance door of every guest room.

Minn. Stat. 327.73 subd. 3 provides that a person who remains in a hotel after having been requested to leave for the reasons stated above is guilty of a misdemeanor. Minn. Stat. 327.73 clearly allows for an Innkeeper to remove guests without being required to bring a court action to enforce the eviction.

Minn. Stat. 327.73 does NOT apply to occupancy that is not considered "transient occupancy". It only applies to a Guest or "other person" which transient occupancy.

Since Minn. Stat. 327.73 only applies to Guests or Transient occupants, it is a reasonable conclusion that it does NOT apply to occupants who are NOT transient occupants. If it is NOT a "transient" occupancy, then Minn. Stat. 504B applies to this situation. This would require Plaintiff to bring an eviction action to evict Defendant from the property and would make it unlawful to lock Plaintiff out.

For a case dealing with this issue see unpublished case titled *William G. Stone vs. Shawn Clow, (A13-0984) Minn. Court of Appeals.* In that case the court held that the determination of whether Clow and Stone had a landlord-tenant or innkeeper-guest relationship is based on the particular circumstances and facts of their relationship; it is not based on whether Riverside Suites has a license to operate as a hotel. See Asseltyne v. Fay Hotel, 222 Minn. 91, 99, 23 N.W.2d 357, 362 (1946). The court in the Stone case held as follows:

To determine whether Clow and Stone had a landlord-tenant or an innkeeper-guest relationship, we look to the specific circumstances of their particular relationship. Asseltyne, 222 Minn. at 99, 23 N.W.2d at 362 (considering whether plaintiff and defendant's relationship was that of innkeeper-guest or that of a proprietor and residential lodger to determine the duty that defendant owed to plaintiff). "The length of the stay, the existence of a special contract, the rate or method of payment, and the possession or nonexistence of a home or permanent residence elsewhere are all material, but not necessarily controlling, factors to be considered in determining the question." Id. (quotations omitted).

The innkeeper statute that Clow cites provides further guidance. A "hotel" is "a hotel, . . or other building, which is a place where sleeping or housekeeping accommodations are supplied for pay to guests for transient occupancy." Minn. Stat. § 327.70, subd. 3 (2012) (emphasis added). "Transient occupancy" means "occupancy when it is the intention of the parties that the occupancy will be temporary." Id., subd. 5 (2012). The statute further provides that a rebuttable presumption is established that the occupancy is not transient "if the unit occupied is the sole residence of the guest." Id.

Applying these principles, we conclude that the district court correctly ruled that a landlord-tenant relationship existed between Clow and Stone. Even recognizing that Riverside Suites operated as a hotel for some guests, the undisputed facts concerning Stone show that the rental unit at Riverside Suites was his only residence, creating a rebuttable presumption that his occupancy was not transient. Stone was in college, he intended to rent the unit until the end of the semester, he moved all his belongings into the rental unit, and he had nowhere else to live after he was locked out of Riverside Suites.

32. Housing Inspector's Report

504B.385 Subd. 6.   **"Hearing.** A certified copy of an inspection   report meets the requirements of rule 803(8) of the Minnesota   Rules of Evidence as an exception to the rule against hearsay,   and meets the requirements of rules 901 and 902 of the Minnesota Rules of Evidence as to authentication."

33. In Forma Pauperis

In Housing Court there are numerous requests for IFP waiver of filing fees.

There are three statutory requirements which must be satisfied before an IFP application may be granted. **First,** the applicant must be a natural person. Corporations, partnerships, and other types of entities are not eligible.   **Second,** the applicant must file an affidavit containing substantially the language prescribed by § 563.01, subd. 3.   **Third,** the court must make an affirmative finding that the action is not "of a frivolous nature."

Bases for Denial of an IFP Petition

The two bases for denying an IFP under § 563.01 are:

1.   The court finds that the affidavit is untrue, i.e., the court finds that the applicant is financially able to pay the fees, costs, and security for costs; or

2.   The court finds that the action is frivolous.

The signing judge may make inquiry of the applicant as to the facts in the affidavit to determine if the facts are true. An applicant's claim that the applicant is financially unable to pay need not be accepted at face value.   If an applicant is receiving public assistance, is represented by a legal services or volunteer attorney or has annual income not greater than 125% of the poverty line established under United States Code, title 42, section 9902(2), such applicant meets the financial need requirement.   Such examples are not exclusive and applicants not meeting any of these may nonetheless be eligible if the signing judge determines that they cannot support themselves and also pay court fees.   If the signing judge determines that the affidavit is untrue, the application must be denied.   A review of the complaint may reveal conflicting information.   For example, an IFP affidavit filed by a Plaintiff may indicate that the affiant does not own real property, but the cause of the action is an eviction case. This is inconsistent and further inquiries need to be made.

The signing judge must also make a determination that the action is not frivolous. The Minnesota Court of Appeals has defined a frivolous claim as one "without any reasonable basis in law or equity and [which] could not be supported by a good faith argument for [a] . . . modification or reversal of existing law." Maddox v. Department of Human Services, 400 N.W.2d 136 (Minn. Ct. App. 1987).

The United States Supreme Court has held that an in forma pauperis complaint "is frivolous [under 28 U.S.C. Section 1915(d)] where it lacks an arguable basis either in law or in fact." Neitzke v. Williams, 490 U.S. 319, 325 (1991).

The U.C. Code under 28 U.S.C. Section 1915(d) gives the courts "the unusual power to pierce the veil of the complaint's factual allegations and dismiss those claims whose factual contentions are clearly baseless." Id. at 327. Thus, the court is not bound, as it usually is when making a determination based solely on the pleadings, to accept without question the truth of the plaintiff's allegations.   However, "the initial assessment of the in forma pauperis plaintiff's factual allegations must be weighted in the plaintiff's favor." Denton v. Hernandez, 504 U.S. 25, 112 S. Ct. 1728, 118 L.Ed.2d 340 (1992).

The Minnesota Legislature and the United States Congress, in enacting IFP statutes, have sought to lower the judicial access barriers to the indigent.   Nonetheless, they have recognized that a litigant whose filing fees and court costs are assumed by the public, unlike a paying litigant, lacks an economic incentive to refrain from filing frivolous, malicious, or repetitive lawsuits.   In response to this concern, the statute allows the courts to deny or dismiss an in forma pauperis complaint if satisfied that the action is frivolous. Minnesota District Court judges are granted broad discretion in deciding IFP applications and will not be reversed except for abuse of discretion. Maddox v. Department of Human Services, 400 N.W.2d 136 (Minn. Ct. App. 1987).

In making an IFP determination, the court must exercise its discretion. As with any exercise of discretion, there are no concrete guidelines. Although § 563.01, subd. 3 requires the applicant's affidavit to state the nature of the action, defense or appeal, the better practice is for the signing judge to review a copy of the pleading to be filed, where one has been prepared. In making such a determination it is not necessary that the court take notice only of facts which can be judicially noticed. A finding of factual frivolousness is appropriate when the facts alleged arise to the level of the irrational or the wholly incredible, whether or not there are judicially noticeable facts available to contradict them. Denton v. Hernandez, 504 U.S. 25, 112 S. Ct. 1728, 118 L.Ed.2d 340 (1992).

Moreover, courts may consider other complaints filed by the applicant. In Denton v. Hernandez, the lower court determined that respondent Hernandez' claims appeared to be "wholly fanciful." While each complaint in that case, taken separately, was not necessarily frivolous, the five complaints taken together told a different story. Respondent claimed he was drugged and attacked by inmates and guards in different institutions over a period of three years yet the modus operandi of the alleged attackers was the same in each case. It is appropriate therefore in the case of "frequent fliers" to inquire of the applicant what other actions have been brought. Understanding the nature of the other claims may lead to a determination that the present action is frivolous.

Procedure for Appeal of IFP Denial

While denial of an application for IFP status is not specifically listed among the orders from which an appeal may be taken, an applicant who has been denied IFP status may appeal pursuant to Minn. R. Civ. App. P. 103.03:

> An appeal may be taken to the Court of Appeals:
> . . .
> (e) from an order which, in effect, determines the action and prevents a judgment from which an appeal might be taken.

In order for an applicant to obtain an appeal, and order denying the application should be entered. It has been the practice in Hennepin County for the signing judge not to enter an order denying IFP status (and instead merely refusing to sign the authorization). The practice has resulted in applicants occasionally seeking out other judges and the chief judge until a favorable ruling is obtained. Applicants dissatisfied with the denial of IFP status by the signing judge typically return to the Civil Intake counter and are referred to the chief judge.

A better procedure would be for the signing judge to enter a written order denying the application for IFP status. The applicant could then perfect an appeal and the judge shopping element could be eliminated.

The section from the Signing Judge Guidelines notebook dealing with IFPs is attached. These guidelines recommend that the judge review not only the affidavit, but also the complaint in order to determine frivolousness and/or indigency, ask additional questions and review the statute before signing or denying any IFP order. The Guidelines also provide names and numbers of three individuals to call if the signing judge has concerns or questions.

New Law Affecting Inmates

In 1995, a revision was added to Minn. Stat. Ch. 563 providing that an inmate who wishes to commence a civil action by proceeding in forma pauperis must meet certain additional requirements. These include: exhausting inmate complaint procedures and authorizing the Commissioner of Corrections to withdraw from the inmate's account the amount advanced or waived by the court until the fees and costs have been paid in full.

Advancement or waiver of additional costs, such as transcripts, expert witness fees, and deposition costs, by the county will be made only upon an order from the judge assigned to this case. Each request must be specifically approved and found to be necessary by you.

Minn. Stat. § 563.01, subd. 10 provides:

> Judgment may be rendered for costs at the conclusion of the action as in other cases. In the event any person recovers moneys by either settlement or judgment as a result of commencing or defending an action in forma pauperis, the costs deferred and the expenses directed by the court to be paid under this sectional shall be included in such moneys and shall be paid directly to the court administrator by the opposing party.

In light of this subdivision, please remind all parties that any settlement in favor of the IFP litigant must include a reimbursement to the district court administrator for costs deferred. Further, it is the responsibility of the judge to incorporate these amounts into any judgment in favor of the IFP litigant.

Sample wording for a judgment in an action where the IFP litigant prevails:

> Pursuant to Minn. Stat. § 563.01, subd. 10, the District Court Administrator is hereby awarded judgment against _____ (the opposing party), in the amount of _____, such amount representing the costs and expenses deferred or advanced in this matter to _____(the IFP party).

Initial Filings. The proper forms are an affidavit and order for proceeding in forma pauperis waiving the initial filing fees, service and publication fees and copying fees only. This order does not and should not allow other costs, such as transcripts, witness fees or depositions.

Subsequent Filings. Once a file has been opened or a matter heard, any subsequent IFP requests must go to the assigned judge or referee who heard the case. These requests must be on a form entitled Supplemental Affidavit for Proceeding In Forma Pauperis. The Signing Judge does not sign these orders.

Frivolous Actions. Subd. 3 of the statute provides that upon a finding by the court that the action is not of a frivolous nature, the court shall allow the person to proceed in forma pauperis. In other words, a frivolous lawsuit is valid reason for refusing to sign an IFP petition. You may want to ask additional questions of the petitioner and ask to read the complaint. Many judges also routinely ask the affiant whether they have been denied this IFP order by another judge.

Denials. Denial of an Order for Proceeding In Forma Pauperis is appealable under Minnesota Rule of Civil Appellate Procedure 103.03(e).

Actions Brought By Prisoners. A 1995 amendment to Minn. Stat. § 563.02 provides for certain procedures to be followed by prisoners seeking IFPs to commence civil actions.

Form Content. The IFP petition should be complete and legible. If it is not on the standard preprinted from, read carefully to make sure that the petitioner has not included extras such as expert witness fees, transcripts, deposition costs, etc. Such requests cannot be approved by the signing judge. They should be submitted on a "Supplemental Affidavit for Proceeding In Forma Pauperis" and should go to the District Court Administrator who will forward it to the trial judge, once the case is assigned.

Transcripts. Requests for payment of transcripts should not be included in the initial IFP. As indicated above, they are properly filed in a supplemental affidavit either with the court administrator and trial judge in the case of deposition transcripts or with the appellate court for a case on appeal.

34. Jury Trial

There is right to a Jury Trial in eviction actions. (Minn. Stat. 504B.335 (b).

There is **NO** right to a Jury trial in rent escrow actions. (Minn. Stat. 504B.385 (subd. 6).

There is **NO** right to a Jury Trial in Tenant Remedy Actions. (Minn. Stat. 504B.421).

Minn. Stat. 504B.351 and 504B.355 talk jury trials in Housing Court cases. Minn. Stat. 504B.351 states that is the jury cannot agree upon a verdict, the court may discharge the members and issue an order impaneling a new jury, immediately or as agreed to by the parties or fixed by the court.

Minn. Stat. 504B.355 states that a verdict of the jury or the finding of the court in favor of the plaintiff in an eviction action shall be substantially in the following form:

> **At a court held at ....., on the ..... day of ....., year ....., before ....., a judge in and for the county of ..... in an action between ....., plaintiff, and ....., defendant, the jury find that the facts alleged in the complaint are true, and the plaintiff shall recover possession of the premises and the defendant(s) shall vacate the premises immediately.**

If the verdict or finding is for the defendant, it shall be sufficient for the Jury to find that the facts alleged in the complaint are not true.

35. Late payment fees

In leases, late fees based upon a breach of the lease payment are generally in the form of liquidated damages, *see Local 34 State, County & Mun. Employees v. County of Hennepin*, 310 Minn. 283, 288, 246 N.W.2d 41, 44 (1976) (*dictum*); and not an unenforceable penalty. *See Palace Theatre, Inc. v. Northwest Theatres Circuit, Inc.*, 186 Minn. 548, 553, 243 N.W. 849, 851 (1932).

Generally, liquidated damages serve as a reasonable forecast of general damages resulting from a breach. *Zirinsky v. Sheehan*, 413 F.2d 481, 485 (8th Cir. 1969), *cert. denied*, 396 U.S. 1059 (1970). The controlling factor is whether the amount agreed upon is reasonable or unreasonable in light of the contract as a whole, the nature of the damages contemplated, and the surrounding circumstances, and <u>not</u> the intention of the parties nor their expression of intention. *Gorco Const. Co. v. Stein*, 256 Minn. 476, 481-82, 99 N.W.2d 69, 74 (1959) (emphasis added). *See Meuwissen v. H.E. Westerman Lumber*, 218 Minn. 477, 483, 16 N.W.2d 546, 549-50 (1944).

In the 2010 Legislative Session, Minn. Stat. 504B.177 was added (effective January 1, 2011) which states that a landlord of a **residential** building may not charge a late fee if the rent is paid after the due date, unless the tenant and landlord have agreed **in writing** that a late fee may be imposed. The agreement must specify when the late fee will be imposed. **In no case may the late fee exceed eight percent** (8%) of the overdue rent payment. For purposes of this paragraph, the "due date" does not include a date, earlier than the date contained in the written or oral lease by which, if the rent is paid, the tenant earns a discount.

If a federal statute, regulation, or handbook providing for late fees for a tenancy subsidized under a federal program conflicts with paragraph (a), then the landlord may continue to publish and implement a late payment fee schedule that complies with the federal statute, regulation, or handbook.

In a Minnesota Court of Appeals Case titled *Housing and Redevelopment Authority of Duluth vs. Brian Lee, file A12-2078,* the court held that the eight percent limitation on late fees that landlords of residential buildings may charge under Minn. Stat. 504B.177 (2010) is not preempted by federal law regarding public housing authorities, as set forth in 42 U.S.C. section1437d(1)(2) (2012) and 24 C.F.R. section 966.4(b)(3) (2013). The Court of Appeals basically said that the public housing authority failed to establish that the eight percent limitation of late fees conflicts with any federal statute.

36. Military Service Members

Active Military Service Members are protected in eviction actions under Title 50, Appendix, War and National Defense, Section 531 of Title III Servicemembers Civil Relief Act.

Under this law, **except by court order**, a landlord may not evict a servicemember, or the dependents of a servicemember, during a period of military service of the servicemember, from premises

> (1) that are occupied or intended to be occupied primarily as a residence; and
> (2) for which the monthly rent does not exceed $2,400, as adjusted under paragraph (2) for years after 2003;

Upon an application for eviction or distress with respect to premises covered by this section, the court may on its own motion and shall, if a request is made by or on behalf of a servicemember whose ability to pay the agreed rent is materially affected by military service—

> (1) stay the proceedings for a period of 90 days, unless in the opinion of the court, justice and equity require a longer or shorter period of time; or
> (2) adjust the obligation under the lease to preserve the interests of all parties.

Relief to landlord- If a stay is granted under Servicemember's Civil Relief Act, the court may grant to the landlord (or other person with paramount title) such relief as equity may require.

37. Minnesota Statutes 555.08- Writ allowed

Minnesota Statutes 555.08 (titled Supplemental Relief) states as follows:

Further relief based on a declaratory judgment or decree may be granted whenever necessary or proper. The application therefor shall be by petition to a court having jurisdiction to grant the relief. If the application be deemed sufficient, the court shall, on reasonable notice, require any adverse party whose rights have been adjudicated by the declaratory judgment or decree, to show cause why further relief should not be granted forthwith.

In the unpublished case titled Arnold F. Koenig vs. Michael A. Koenig, defendant and third party plaintiff vs. Andrea Koenig and the Koenig Farm Corporation, the Court of Appeals addressed the issue of whether or not a Judge could issue a Writ or Recover and evict a party from property under Minn. Stat. 555.08. The court in that decision wrote as follows:

> *Appellants argue that the district court erred by permitting respondents to seek eviction and a writ of recovery as supplemental relief, under Minn. Stat. § 555.08, rather than requiring them to commence a separate eviction action under chapter 504B. Statutory interpretation is a question of law, which we review de novo. Krueger v. Zeman Constr. Co., 781 N.W.2d 858, 861 (Minn. 2010). "The object of all interpretation and construction of laws is to ascertain and effectuate the intention of the legislature." Minn. Stat. § 645.16 (2010). "When the words of a law in their application to an existing situation are clear and free from all ambiguity, the letter of the law shall not be disregarded under the pretext of pursuing the spirit." Id.*

> *Appellants allege that because chapter 504B authorizes eviction actions and contains procedural requirements, a party is precluded from seeking eviction under the authority of section 555.08. We disagree.*

> *Minnesota Statutes section 555.08 authorizes a district court to grant further relief based on a declaratory judgment or decree.*

> *Aside from these limited requirements, the statute does not limit the relief that a court may grant. Moreover, appellants neither point to language in section 555.08 or chapter 504B nor any authority interpreting either statute that supports their assertion that chapter 504B precludes eviction as supplemental relief under section 555.08. **We conclude therefore that the district court did not err by permitting respondents to seek eviction and a writ of recovery as supplemental relief under section 555.08.***

38. Mistakes

Housing court has a lot of pro se parties and as a result, you will discover a lot of mistakes in the pleadings and service. There are at least three rules that allow the court discretion in addressing these mistakes.

Rule 4.07- Amendments

The court in its discretion and on such terms as it deems just may at any time allow any summons or other process or proof of service thereof to be amended, unless it clearly appears that substantial rights of the person against whom the process issued would be prejudiced thereby.

Rule 6.02 Enlargement of time requirements

When by statute, by these rules, by a notice given thereunder, or by order of court an act is required or allowed to be done at or within a specified time, the court for cause shown may, at any time in its discretion, (1) with or without motion or notice order the period enlarged if request therefor is made before the expiration of the period originally prescribed or as extended by a previous order, or (2) upon motion made after the expiration of the specified period permit the act to be done where the failure to act was the result of excusable neglect; but it may not extend the time for taking any action under Rules 4.043, 59.03, 59.05, and 60.02 except to the extent and under the conditions stated in them.

Rule 60.02- Mistakes; Inadvertence; Excusable Neglect; Newly Discovered Evidence; Fraud; etc

On motion and upon such terms as are just, the court may relieve a party or the party's legal representatives from a final judgment (other than a marriage dissolution decree), order, or proceeding and may order a new trial or grant such other relief as may be just for the following reasons:

(a) Mistake, inadvertence, surprise, or excusable neglect;
(b) Newly discovered evidence which by due diligence could not have been discovered in time to move for a new trial pursuant to Rule 59.03;
(c) Fraud (whether heretofore denominated intrinsic or extrinsic), misrepresentation, or other misconduct of an adverse party;
(d) The judgment is void;
(e) The judgment has been satisfied, released, or discharged or a prior judgment upon which it is based has been reversed or otherwise vacated, or it is no longer equitable that the judgment should have prospective application; or
(f) Any other reason justifying relief from the operation of the judgment.

39. Mobile Homes.

Mobile home eviction actions are governed by both Minn. Chapter 504B and Minn. Stat. 327C.09.

10 day Notice Requirement

Generally, in addition to the Eviction action notice periods, **Landlords must give an additional 10 days written notice to the resident and any party holding a security interest** in the mobile home that a periodic rental or utilities payment owed to the mobile park owner is overdue. The Landlord may then bring an eviction action if neither the resident nor the secured party cures the default within ten days of receiving the notice.

30 day Notice Requirement

The additional ten day notice requirement applies to all non payment of rent cases. However, Minn. Stat. 327C.09 requires that a **30 day notice** be given for other violations of the mobile home rules, including Subd. 3. Violations of local ordinance, state law or state rule relating to manufactured homes; Subd. 4. Rule violations; and Subd. 5, if the resident acts in the park in a manner which endangers other residents or park personnel, causes substantial damage to the park premises or substantially annoys other residents.

If the breach is for nonpayment of rent, then the ten day notice must be given to both the resident and any party holding a security interest in the mobile home. For the other breaches where a 30 day notice is required, the notice only has to be given to the Resident. The exception to the 30 day notice is if this is the second violation after receipt of the first notice of violation.

To be effective, the notice must specify the time, date, and nature of the alleged annoyance, damage, or endangerment. A park owner seeking to evict pursuant to this subdivision need not produce evidence of a criminal conviction, even if the alleged misconduct constitutes a criminal offense.

Right to Redeem

Under Minn. Stat. 327C.11 subd. 1, the resident in a mobile home eviction action has the right to redeem. This right of redemption, as expressed in section 504B.291 and the common law, is available to a resident from whom a park owner seeks to recover possession for nonpayment of rent, but no resident may exercise that right more than twice in any 12-month period; provided, that a resident may exercise the right of redemption more than twice in any 12-month period by paying the park owner's actual reasonable attorney's fees as part of each additional exercise of that right during the 12-month period.

Waiver of Notice by Accepting Rent

A park owner who gives a resident a notice as provided in section 327C.09, subdivision 3, 4, 6, or 8, or 327C.095, does not waive the notice by afterwards accepting rent. **However,** acceptance of rent for a period after the expiration of a final notice to quit waives that notice unless the parties agree in writing after service of the notice that the notice continues in effect.

Writs and Conditional Writs for Mobile Homes

The issuance of a writ of restitution, other than a conditional writ, shall be stayed for a reasonable period not to exceed seven days to allow the resident to arrange to remove the resident's home from the lot. Under Minn. Stat. 327C.11 the court may issue a **conditional writ.** Where the interests of justice require the court may issue a conditional writ of restitution, which orders the resident and all those in the resident's household to stop residing in the park within a reasonable period not to exceed seven days, but which allows the resident's home to remain on the lot for 60 days for the purpose of an in park sale, as provided in section 327C.07. The writ shall also direct the park owner to notify any party holding a security interest in the resident's home and known to the park owner, of the provisions of the writ. If the court issues a conditional writ, the resident may keep the home on the lot for 60 days for an in park sale if:

a)   neither the resident nor members of the resident's household reside in the park;

b)   the resident complies with all rules relating to home and lot maintenance; and

c)   the resident pays on time all rent and utility charges owed to the park owner. If the resident fails to meet any of these conditions, the park owner may, on three days' written notice to the resident, move the court for an order making the writ of restitution unconditional. Sixty-one days after the issuance of a conditional writ, the writ shall become absolute without further court action.

40. Mortgage Foreclosures

Minn. Stat. 504B.285 provides that Plaintiffs may recover possession of property by eviction when any person holds over real property: (1) after the sale of property on an execution of judgment **(2) on foreclosure of a mortgage and expiration of the time for redemption;** (3) after termination of a contract for deed (4) upon breach of a lease or (5) after termination of a tenancy by notice to quit.

Minnesota Statutes 580.12 provides that when so recorded, upon expiration of the time for redemption, the **Certificate of Sale** prepared by the Sheriff shall operate as a conveyance to the purchaser or the purchaser's assignee of all the right, title, and interest of the mortgagor in and to the premises named therein at the date of such mortgage, without any other conveyance.

In 2009, Congress passed Plaintiff 111-22 Title VII- **Protecting Tenants at Foreclosure Act.** This act is effective until December 31, 2012 and goes into effect on any case where the foreclosure process was commenced after May, 2009.

In 2010, Minnesota amended Minn. Stat. 504B.285 which provides (for evictions that occur prior to January 1, 2013) that where a person in possession of foreclosed property **has a bona fide lease** the successor in interest to the property must provide to the Tenant at least 90 days written notice on the date the redemption period ends and lasts at least 90 days after the expiration of the time for redemption, **provided that Tenant pays the rent** and abides by all terms of the lease.

If the eviction action is commenced prior to December 31, 2012, the Tenant must be allowed to stay until the end of the term lease upon 90 days notice **unless** the successor in interest is going to occupy the residence.

This act basically requires, under most circumstances, (up to January 1, 2013) for Landlords to give Tenants at least 90 days written notice to vacate in foreclosures if the lease is bona fide and Tenants pay the rent due under their bona fide lease.

Issues that the court may need to address are whether or not the lease is a **bona fide lease**. There is of course common law definitions of what constitutes bona fide. Minn. Stat. 504B.285 also states that a lease or tenancy shall be considered bona fide only if:

1) the mortgagor, or the spouse, child, or parent of the mortgagor is not the Tenant.
2) the lease was the result of an arms length transaction and
3) the rent paid is not substantially less than the fair market value of property.

In summary then, in foreclosure situations, Tenants with bona fide leases have the right to remain in the property provided they pay the rent due and comply with the terms of the bona fide lease. If the lease is a Section 8 lease, then the successor in interest or Bank takes possession subject to the Section 8 voucher lease and Housing Authority assistance payments. If the lease is bona fide and has a term longer than 90 days, and if the successor in interest does not intend to reside in the property, the Tenant could be allowed to stay in the property until the end of the term.

Effective January 1, 2013, the notice period for foreclosures will be reduced to two months, provided Tenant pays rent and abides by lease.

41. Nuisance.

A Prosecuting Attorney or the owner of the property may bring an action against a rental property under the Nuisance law under Minn. Stat. 617.81. Actions could involve canceling the lease and eviction or enjoining the use of the building for one year!

Acts constituting a nuisance. (a) For purposes of sections 617.80 to 617.87, a public nuisance exists upon proof of two or more separate behavioral incidents of one or more of the following, committed within the previous 12 months within the building:

(1) prostitution or prostitution-related activity committed within the building;
(2) gambling or gambling-related activity committed within the building;
(3) maintaining a public nuisance in violation of section 609.74, clause (1) or (3); [20]
(4) permitting a public nuisance in violation of section 609.745; [21]
(5) unlawful sale, possession, storage, delivery, giving, manufacture, cultivation, or use of controlled substances committed within the building;
(6) unlicensed sales of alcoholic beverages committed within the building in violation of

---

[20] **609.74 PUBLIC NUISANCE.**
Whoever by an act or failure to perform a legal duty intentionally does any of the following is guilty of maintaining a public nuisance, which is a misdemeanor:
(1) maintains or permits a condition which unreasonably annoys, injures or endangers the safety, health, morals, comfort, or repose of any considerable number of members of the public; or
(2) interferes with, obstructs, or renders dangerous for passage, any public highway or right-of-way, or waters used by the public; or
(3) is guilty of any other act or omission declared by law to be a public nuisance and for which no sentence is specifically provided.

[21] **609.745 PERMITTING PUBLIC NUISANCE.**
Whoever having control of real property permits it to be used to maintain a public nuisance or lets the same knowing it will be so used is guilty of a misdemeanor.

section <u>340A.401</u>;

(7) unlawful sales or gifts of alcoholic beverages by an unlicensed person committed within the building in violation of section <u>340A.503, subdivision 2</u>, clause (1);

(8) unlawful use or possession of a firearm in violation of section <u>609.66, subdivision 1a</u>,

<u>609.67</u>, or <u>624.713</u>, committed within the building; or

(9) violation by a commercial enterprise of local or state business licensing regulations,

ordinances, or statutes prohibiting the maintenance of a public nuisance as defined in section <u>609.74</u> or the control of a public nuisance as defined in section <u>609.745</u>.

If the building contains more than one rental unit, two or more behavioral incidents must consist of conduct:

(1) anywhere in the building by the same tenant or lessee, or persons acting in conjunction with or under the control of the same tenant or lessee;

(2) by any persons within the same rental unit while occupied by the same tenant or lessee or within two or more rental units while occupied by the same tenant or lessee; or

(3) by the owner of the building or persons acting in conjunction with or under the control of the owner.

42. Parol Evidence.

The question of whether the parties entered into an oral modification of the contract is a question of fact. *See Johnson v. Quaal,* 250 Minn. 154, 158, 83 N.W.2d 796, 799 (1957). A court may consider **parol evidence** of subsequent conversations that alter the terms of a contract to determine if the parties have orally modified a contract. <u>*Nord v. Herreid,* 305 N.W.2d 337, 339-40 (Minn.1981)</u>. The parties' written contract provides that "[a]ny alteration or deviation from above specifications involving extra costs will be executed only upon written orders." But under Minnesota law, parties may agree to orally modify a contract, even if the contract contains a provision requiring that modifications be in writing. <u>*See Larson v. Hill's Heating & Refrig. of Bemidji,* 400 N.W.2d 777, 781 (Minn.App.1987)</u> (acknowledging general common-law rule that "a written contract can be varied or rescinded by oral agreement of the parties, even if the contract provides that it shall not be orally varied or rescinded" and determining that parties' agreement to terminate employment contract was effective despite contract's provision against oral modification), *review denied* (Minn. Apr. 17, 1987).

Other Minnesota Cases which address the issue of parol evidence: The aim of contract interpretation is to determine and enforce the intent of the parties. <u>Motorsports Racing Plus, Inc., v. Arctic Cat Sales, Inc.</u>, 666 N.W.2d 320, 323 (Minn.2003). If the contract's language is clear and unambiguous, the court should not "rewrite, modify, or limit its effect by a strained construction." Travertine Corp. v. Lexington-Silverwood, 683 N.W.2d 267, 271 (Minn.2004). If the language is incomplete or ambiguous, evidence relevant to the intent of the parties-parol evidence-may be considered. Material Movers, Inc. v. Hill, 316 N.W.2d 13, 17 (Minn.1982).

43. Power of Attorney

Rule 603 of the Housing Court Rules states that an unlawful detainer action shall be brought in the name of the owner of the property or other person entitled to possession of the premises. No agent shall sue in the agent's own name. Any agent suing for a principal shall attach a copy of the Power of Authority to the complaint at the time of filing. No person other than a principal or a duly licensed lawyer shall be allowed to appear in Housing Court unless the Power of Authority is attached to the complaint at the time of filing, and no person other than a duly licensed lawyer shall be allowed to appear unless the Power of Authority is so attached to the complaint. An agent or lay advocate may appear without a written Power of Authority if the party being so represented is an individual and is also present at the hearing

44. Public Housing

Public or government subsidized tenancies fall into four categories:

1. Housing owned and operated by agency such as Minneapolis Public Housing Authority. Rent tied to income.
2. Programs which provide federal funds directly to Landlords in connection with the building, renovation or operation of subsidized units. Rent tied to income.
3. Properties which have received money from the Federal Low Income Housing Tax Credit program. In these units, Tenants may not know they are in low income housing. Their rent is not tied to their income.
4. Section 8 Voucher programs in which private Landlord's received subsidy. Rent Tenant pays is tied to income. Landlord received full rent, a portion from HUD and a portion from Tenant.

A lease for public housing may only be terminated by the landlord for "**serious or repeated violation of material terms of the lease**," exceeding income requirements, or other good cause. 24 C.F.R. § 966.4(l)(2). The federal regulation provides two examples of a serious and repeated violation of a material term of the lease: "failure to make payments due under the lease; and failure to fulfill household obligations, as described in paragraph (f) of this section." 24 C.F.R. § 966.4(l)(2)(i)(A), (B). Paragraph (f) lists the tenant's obligations that shall be contained in the lease. 24 C .F.R. § 966.4(f).   In relevant part, the federal regulations state that the tenant shall be obligated:

- To abide by necessary and reasonable regulations promulgated by the PHA for the benefit and well-being of the housing project and the tenants which shall be posted in the project office and incorporated by reference in the lease;

-To comply with all obligations imposed upon tenants by applicable provisions of building and housing codes materially affecting health and safety;

-To act, and cause household members or guests to act, in a manner which will not disturb other residents' peaceful enjoyment of their accommodations and will be conducive to maintaining the project in a decent, safe, and sanitary condition.

The materiality of a breach is a question of fact. Cloverdale Foods, 580 N.W.2d at 49-50. A breach is material when "one of the primary purposes" of a contract is violated.   Steller v. Thomas, 232 Minn. 275, 282, 286-87, 45 N.W.2d 537, 542, 544 (1950); see also Samuel Williston & Richard A. Lord, A Treatise on the Law of Contracts § 44:55 (4th ed.2000) (stating that material breach "goes to the root or essence of the contract").

45. Redemption Right.

Tenants have an absolute right to redeem the tenancy by paying the rent in arrears with interest, costs of the action, attorney's fees not to exceed $5, and performing any other obligations of the lease.   Minn. Stat. 504B.291.   This right of redemption terminates on the date and exact time allowed by the court.   See LaMac Cleaners, Inc. vs. Paul Jasa et al (C4-02-1239, 2003 (unpublished case).   In that case the Court held as follows:

> Following a hearing on June 11th, the district court found in favor of the plaintiff landlord. But the court did not immediately enter judgment and issue a writ of recovery and premises and order to vacate. Instead, as permitted by Minn. Stat. 504B.345, subd. 1(d), the court gave appellant until 9:00 a.m. on June 13 to redeem the property by paying respondent $1,928 and directed that if appellant failed to do so, a judgment and writ would issue by default. At 9:00 a.m. on June 13, the court's stay of its order ended, and because appellant had not paid the rent, a judgment and writ issued by default.

> Appellant argues that it substantially complied with the district court's redemption order because it was prepared to and fully intended to pay the rent at 9:10 a.m. But under this court's reasoning in McCusker, the court's signed order became effective at 9:00 a.m. and therefore, the redemption period ended at 9:00 a.m.

It should be noted that the redemption right limits the amount of Attorney fees that Tenants are required to pay. Also, this redemption right applies to commercial as well as residential leases.   If a commercial lease allows Landlord attorney fees for a breach, then Landlord will need to pursue payment of the attorney fees in a separate action for breach of contract, and cannot evict the Tenant so long as Tenant pays the rent due and the $5.00 in attorney fees required by this statute.   Redemption rights for mobile home evictions are a little different (See Mobile Homes Above).

46. Rent Abatement.

Under Minn.Stat. § 504B.425(a), (e) (2000), if the court finds that a violation of clause (1) or (2) of Minn.Stat. 504B.161, subd. 1[22], has been proved, in its discretion, the court may find the extent to which any uncorrected violations impair the residential tenants' use and enjoyment of the property contracted for and order the rent abated accordingly.   If the court enters judgment under this paragraph, the parties shall be informed and the court shall determine the amount by which the rent is to be abated. See also Minn.Stat. §§ 504B.395, subd. 1(1) (procedure for bringing tenants' action), 504B.001, subd. 14(2) (2000) (defining violation).

Under this statute, the court has discretion to order rent abatement; it is not required to order abatement. Compare Minn.Stat. § 645.44, subd. 15 (2000) (stating " 'may' is permissive") with Minn.Stat. § 645.44, subd. 16 (2000) (stating " 'shall' is mandatory"). Under both Minn.Stat. § 566.25 and Minn.Stat. § 566.34, subd. 10, the district court "may, in its discretion," order one or more of several possible remedies including rent abatement. Minn.Stat. §§ 566.25(d); 566.34, subd. 10(a)(1). The statutes' use of "may" combined with their non-exclusive lists of remedies show that no particular remedy is mandatory and that the district court has broad discretion to select the remedy appropriate to the facts of the case. *Compare Minn.Stat. § 645.44, subd. 15 (1994) (" [m]ay' is permissive") with Minn.Stat. § 645.44, subd. 16 (1994) (" '[s]hall' is mandatory").   Scroggins v. Solchaga 552 N.W. 2d 248, (Minn. App. 1996).*

---

[22]   **504B.161 Covenants of landlord or licensor.**

Subdivision 1.   **Requirements.** In every lease or license of residential premises, the landlord or licensor covenants:

(1) that the premises and all common areas are fit for the use intended by the parties;

(2) to keep the premises in reasonable repair during the term of the lease or license, except when the disrepair has been caused by the willful, malicious, or irresponsible conduct of the tenant or licensee or a person under the direction or control of the tenant or licensee; and

(3) to maintain the premises in compliance with the applicable health and safety laws of the state, including the weatherstripping, caulking, storm window, and storm door energy efficiency standards for renter-occupied residences prescribed by section 216C.27, subdivisions 1 and 3, and of the local units of government where the premises are located during the term of the lease or license, except when violation of the health and safety laws has been caused by the willful, malicious, or irresponsible conduct of the tenant or licensee or a person under the direction or control of the tenant or licensee.

The parties to a lease or license of residential premises may not waive or modify the covenants imposed by this section.

47. Rent Escrow

Rent Escrow actions in Housing Court are covered by Minn. Stat. 504B.385, which states that if a code violation exists in a residential building, a residential tenant may deposit the amount of rent due to a Landlord with the court administrator and commence a rent escrow case. The filing fee at the present time is only $70.00 (2010).

A prerequisite to the filing of a rent escrow action is giving Landlord notice of the code violation or repairs that need to be done and allowing Landlord at lease 14 days to do the work. If the repairs are ordered by a Housing Inspector, the Housing Inspector will generally list a completion date for the work to be done. Tenant may commence rent escrow earlier than completion date if asserts time to complete the work excessive.

Tenants may also assert a Fritz defense in an eviction action (see Fritz v. Warthan, 298 Minn. 54, 213 N.W.2d 339). "Fritz" cases are basically rent escrow actions in reverse. In a Fritz defense case, Tenants must deposit the rent owed Landlord also. Regarding this escrow of rent, the Court of Appeals in the "Fritz" case held as follows:

> *Recognizing these potential problems, we have concluded that once the trial court has determined that a fact question exists as to the breach of the covenants of habitability, that court will order the tenant to* **pay the rent to be withheld** *from the landlord into court ...., and that until final resolution on the merits, any future rent withheld shall also be paid into court. The court under its inherent powers may order payment of amounts out of this fund to enable the landlord to make repairs or meet his obligations on the property or for other appropriate purposes. In the majority of cases, final determination of the action will be made quickly and this procedure will not have to be used. It is anticipated that the trial court, in lieu of ordering the rent paid into court, in the exercise of its discretion may order that it be deposited in escrow subject to appropriate terms and conditions or, in lieu of the payment of rents, may require adequate security therefor if such a procedure is more suitable under the circumstances.*

In rent escrow cases under Minn. Stat. 504B.385, the Court has discretion to do any of the following:

    (i) order relief as provided in section 504B.425,[23] including retroactive rent abatement;

---

[23]   **504B.425 Judgment.**

    (a) If the court finds that the complaint in section 504B.395 has been proved, it may, in its discretion, take any of the actions described in paragraphs (b) to (g), either alone or in combination.

    (b) The court may order the landlord to remedy the violation or violations found by the court to exist if the court is satisfied that corrective action will be undertaken promptly.

(ii) order that all or a portion of the rent in escrow be released for the purpose of remedying the violation;

(iii) order that rent be deposited with the court as it becomes due to the landlord or abate future rent until the landlord remedies the violation; or

(iv) impose fines as required in section <u>504B.391</u>.

When a proceeding under this section has been consolidated with a counterclaim for possession or an eviction action, (Fritz defense) and the landlord prevails, the residential tenant may redeem the tenancy as provided in section 504B.291.

In the "Fritz" case, the court **did not** require the residential tenant to pay the landlord's filing fee as a condition of retaining possession of the property when the residential tenant has deposited with the court the full amount of money found by the court to be owed to the landlord.

48. Rental License

Under 504B.385 a Court has discretion to order rent abatement under subd. 9 if it finds that a violation exists as defined under 504B.001 subd. 14. A violation includes any violation of state law or municipal codes related to a rental unit which includes having a rental license.   In a recent unpublished opinion (<u>Beumia vs. Eisenbraun</u>, (A06-1482 Ct. App. 2007) the Minnesota Court of Appeals addressed the issue of a rental license requirement in the City of Alexandria.   **The Alexandria City Ordinance provided that any written or oral agreement to rent any rental unit that did not have a rental license was illegal as a matter of law**. The Court stated as follows:

> *A lessor's compliance with a covenant imposed by law and a lessee's duty to perform under a lease agreement are mutually dependent.* See Fritz v. Warthen, 298 Minn. 54, 58, 213 N.W.2d 339, 341 (1973). Here, Beaumia acquired the house on October 17, 2005, but did not register it with the city as a rental unit until May 23, 2006.

(c) The court may order the residential tenant to remedy the violation or violations found by the court to exist and   deduct the cost from the rent subject to the terms as the court   determines to be just.

(d) The court may appoint an administrator with powers described in section <u>504B.445</u>, and:

(e) Order that rents due in future be deposited with the Court.

> *Thus, the earliest that Beaumia was in compliance with the ordinance was May 23, and before that date, the Eisenbrauns had no obligation to pay rent.*
>
> *When an eviction action is based solely on a failure to pay rent, if a tenant's duty to pay rent was excused, the eviction action fails. In Mac-Du Props. v. LaBresh, 392 N.W.2d 315, 316-17 (Minn. App. 1986), review denied (Minn. Oct. 29, 1986), the landlord failed to acquire a "certificate of occupancy" from the city as required by an ordinance. This court determined that the **landlord's compliance with the ordinance and the tenant's duty to pay rent were mutually dependent.** Id. at 319. Thus, because the tenant was under no duty to pay rent, and because the action was based solely on the tenant's failure to pay rent, the tenant's eviction was improper. Id.*

Under the ruling in the unpublished Court of Appeals decision, therefore, a Tenant in the City of Alexandria had no duty to pay rent until the Landlord had obtained a rental license. This ruling seems to suggest the Landlord could evict for other reasons, but not for failure to pay rent. (at least until the rental licenses has been obtained).

Each city has their own rules regarding rental licenses. Not all cities have the strong language used by the City of Alexandria. Pursuant to this Unpublished Court of Appeals decision, however, there is certainly a reasonable argument that Landlord's can't evict for non payment of rent if Landlord is not in compliance with a City ordinance requiring a rental license. This unpublished decision has persuasive value, but it is not precedential. Dynamic Air, Inc. v. Bloch 502 N.W. 2d 796 (Minn. Ct. App. 1993) also Minn. Stat. 480A.08 subd. 3. Also, the statutory language under Minn. Stat. 504B.385 still seems to suggest that courts have discretion to award rent abatement for a violation of any state or municipal law.

In most cities rental licenses are NOT required when persons rent out rooms in their homestead.

49. Retaliation

Retaliation defenses apply to breach of lease and notice to vacate cases only under Minn. Stat. 504B.285. A retaliation defense does NOT apply to non payment of rent cases under Minn. Stat. 504B.291.

50. Right to Reentry Clause

Tenants will occasionally raise the defense that Landlord may not recover possession of property where the lease does not have a right of re-entry clause. Minn. Stat. 504B.291 states that a Landlord may recover possession based on breach of lease "irrespective of whether the lease contains a right of reentry clause".

In an unpublished case titled C & T Properties v. McCallister (no. C9-98-940 unpublished (Minn Ct. App 1999); the court held as follows:

> In support of her argument that respondent cannot recover possession of the property, McCallister cites Bauer v. Knoble, 51 Minn. 358, 53 N.W. 805 (1892). Bauer concluded that where a lease does not contain a provision for termination of the lease or right of re-entry upon the breach of a covenant, holding over after the breach of a lease covenant "cannot be said to be contrary to the conditions or covenants of the lease." Id. at 359, 53 N.W. 805, 53 N.W. at 805. As a result, the supreme court found that the summary remedy provided by the unlawful detainer statute was unavailable to the landlord. Id. (interpreting Minn. Gen.Stat. ch. 84, § 11 (1878)).

> McCallister argues that the language of the unlawful detainer statute has remained almost unchanged since 1892 and Bauer is, therefore, binding on Minnesota courts, citing Minn.Stat. §§ 645.17(4) (1996) (presuming that, "[w]hen a court of last resort has construed the language of a law," reenactment of statute without change constitutes adoption of construction), 566.03, subd. 1(2) (using language similar to that interpreted in Bauer to describe landlord's rights). McCallister asserts, therefore, that the district court erred in concluding that respondent was entitled to a writ of restitution of the property.

> But McCallister ignores a 1971 addition to the unlawful detainer statute, which provides:

>> *Nothing contained herein shall limit the right of the lessor pursuant to the provisions of subdivision 1 to terminate a tenancy for a violation by the tenant of a lawful, material provision of a lease or contract.*

> Minn.Stat. § 566.03, subd. 4. And this court has stated that "a landlord's right of action for unlawful detainer is complete upon a tenant's violation of a lease condition." Minneapolis Community Dev. Agency, 379 N.W.2d at 556 (citing First Minneapolis Trust Co. v. Lancaster Corp., 185 Minn. 121, 131, 240 N.W. 459, 464 (1931) (involving tenant in default of payment of rent)).

> In First Minneapolis Trust Co., the court noted that the landlord's "right to prosecute [an action for unlawful detainer] is not based upon the right of re-entry contained in the lease." 185 Minn. at 131, 240 N.W. at 464. Consequently, "[t]he provisions in the lease * * * in no way preclude the lessor * * * from pursuing [the] remedy" of unlawful detainer. Id. at 133, 240 N.W. 459, 240 N.W. at 464 (citation omitted). Thus, to maintain an unlawful detainer action, the landlord only "must plead and prove facts which show the [tenant] is in unlawful possession

of [the] property." Mac-Du Properties, 392 N.W.2d at 317 (citing Minn.Stat. § 566.03, subd. 1).

Based on the C & T Properties v. McCallister (no. C9-98-940 unpublished (Minn Ct. App 1999), and the findings in that case, I do not believe an eviction should be denied based on the failure of the lease to have a right of re-entry clause.

51. Section 8 Leases

The federal Section 8 program subsidizes housing for low-income tenants, and is administered by local public housing authorities. 42 U.S.C. § 1437f (2006); 24 C.F.R. § 982.1(a)(1) (2009). The Section 8 program provides two types of assistance, project-based and tenant-based. See 42 U.S.C. § 1437f(d); 24 C.F.R. § 982(b) (2009); Occhino v. Grover, 640 N.W.2d 357, 359 (Minn. App. 2002), review denied (Minn. May 28, 2002). In a tenant-based program, or HCV program, "the family selects a suitable unit. After approving the tenancy, the public housing authority enters into a contract to make rental subsidy payments to the owner to subsidize occupancy by the family." 24 C.F.R. § 982.1(b)(2); see Occhino, 640 N.W.2d at 359 (describing program).

Under federal law, Section 8 is a voluntary program and property owners will be bound by a contract only if "the owner is willing to lease the unit under the program." 24 C.F.R. § 982.302(b) (2009). But "nothing in part 982 is intended to pre-empt operation of [s]tate and local laws that prohibit discrimination against a Section 8 voucher-holder because of status as a Section 8 voucher-holder." 24 C.F.R. § 982.53(d) (2009). Thus, "[t]he Federal statute merely creates the scheme and sets out the guidelines for the funding and implementation of the program . . . through local housing authorities. It does not preclude [s]tate regulation." Attorney Gen. v. Brown, 511 N.E.2d 1103, 1105 (Mass. 1987).

Minnesota law does not require property owners to participate in the Section 8 program. Therefore, a Landlord's refusal to participate in the voluntary Section 8 program for a legitimate business reason does not constitute discrimination under the Minnesota Human Rights Act. See Edwards v. Hopkins Plaza Limited Partnership (Minn. Ct. App 2010 file No. A09-1616).

Service of Section 8 Evictions on the Housing Authority

In Section 8 cases there are three parties involved: Landlord, Tenant, and the Housing Authority. The Housing Authority will rarely be a party to an eviction action. However, in all Section 8 cases the Landlord has a contract with the Housing Authority which states that a Tenancy Addendum (Part C) must be attached to the lease which requires Landlord to serve a copy of the Eviction action on the Housing Authority at the same time the eviction action is served on Tenant. The Tenant has a right to enforce this provision.

Tenants will often ask the Court to dismiss an eviction action involving Section 8 vouchers because Landlord has not served the Housing Authority with a copy of the Summons and Complaint.

If the Housing Authority is not served, Landlord is in violation of the lease requirement that the Housing Authority be served. The question is then raised should the Court 1) dismiss based on this breach, 2) proceed with the eviction action and address this breach at trial, or 3) should the Court require service or joinder as allowed by Rule 19 of the Rules of Civil Procedure?[24] Often the Tenant will admit they are in breach of the lease also by owing rent so you have a situation where both parties are in breach. What is the right thing to do?

A rule in the law of contracts is that a party cannot raise to its advantage a breach of contract against another party when it has first breached the contract itself. MTS vs. Taiga 365 N.W.2d 321 (Minn. App. 1985) Cheezem Development Corp. v. Intracoastal Sales and Service, Inc., 336 So.2d. 1210, 1212 (Fla.Ct.App.1976); Yonan v. Oak Park Federal Savings and Loan Association, 326 N.E.2d 773, 781 (Ill.App.1975); Robinhorne Construction Corp. v. Snyder, 251 N.E.2d 641, 645-46 (Ill.App.1969), aff'd, 265 N.E.2d 670 (Ill.1970). Cf. Verran v. Blacklock, 60 Mich.App. 763, 231 N.W.2d 544, 547 (1975); Odysseys Unlimited, Inc. v. Astral Travel Service, 77 Misc.2d 502, 354 N.Y.S.2d 88, 91 (Sup.Ct.1974). In the Taiga case the rule was applied because in that case Plaintiff's initial breach was a cause of the alleged breach by defendant. Usually in these Landlord Tenant relationships, the failure by the Landlord to notify HUD in violation of the lease is not a "first breach" and usually has no relationship to the breach of tenant which is either breach of lease or non payment of rent.

When a Tenant raises the issue of Landlord not notifying the Housing Authority of the eviction action, the best course of action is to look at the facts on a case by case basis to decide what is fair and equitable under the circumstances. It is obviously important that the Housing Authority know that the Landlord wants to evict the Section 8 Tenant, so the court needs to make sure the Landlord gives the Housing Authority notice. This can be easily done by continuing the case and ordering the Landlord to send notice to the

---

[24] The Code of Federal Regulations require the Landlord to serve notice on the Housing Authority of any eviction action but do not require this notice to be at the time of the commencement of the action. Prior to 1995, 24 C.F.R. §§ 882.215(c)(1) and 887.213(c) provided that the owner must notify the housing authority in writing at the same time that the owner gives notice to the tenant under state or local law. In 1995 this regulation was changed to simply state: "The owner must give the HA [housing authority] a copy of any owner eviction notice to the tenant." 24 C.F.R. § 982.310(e)(2)(ii), 60 Fed. Reg. at 34,705. The time requirement that it be served at the same time was eliminated.

Housing Authority prior to the next court hearing. You could dismiss also if you believe the circumstances justify requiring the Landlord to start all over again.

Landlord and Tenant "Side Deals"

Another issue that comes up often is the situation where the parties will submit a proposed lease to the Housing Authority that has a rent amount that is different from what Landlord expects Tenant to pay. For example, the parties sign a written lease for $1,500.00 per month plus Tenant pays all utilities. Tenant tries to get a Section 8 Voucher and is told by the Housing Authority that Tenant will get a voucher only if the rent is reduced to $1,200.00 and Tenant only pays electric with Landlord paying the balance. Landlord and Tenant then sign a statement requesting the housing assistance which states that the monthly rent is $1,200.00 and Tenant is only paying the electric. Landlord will later bring an eviction action alleging that in truth, Tenant owes the $1,500.00 per month in rent since that is what the original lease states.

It is my position that Landlord is only entitled to receive the rent that Landlord told the Housing Authority was being charged. The parties cannot have side deals since the Housing Authority based its housing benefit on the $1,200.00 per month, NOT the side deal. If Landlord makes a representation to the Housing authority that rent is a certain amount in order to get the government benefit, then Landlord is estopped from charging anything above that amount.

Condition Precedents

There are certain "condition Precedents" in Section 8 HUD leases where Landlord's are required to do certain things prior to commencing an eviction action, including giving Tenant written notices required by HUD regulations which must be done prior to commencement of the eviction action. See case <u>Hoglund-Hall v. Kleinschmidt, 381 N.W.2d 889 (Minn. App. 1986)</u> in which the court dismissed the action because Landlord did not comply with federal housing regulations regarding pre eviction notice.

52. Service of Process

Minn. Stat. 504B.331 governs service of process in eviction cases. In eviction cases only seven days notice is required. Service can be either by personal or substitute service or by posting. If service is by posting, then Plaintiff needs to file four affidavits of service with the court, namely:

  a. Affidavit of Not Found
  b. Affidavit of Posting
  c. Affidavit of Mailing
  d. Affidavit of Plaintiff

Service cannot be avoided by physically refusing to accept a summons where a reasonable person would know that personal service is being attempted. *See* <u>Richard Ochs vs. Elizabeth W. Kimball Esq. et. al.</u> *(Court of Appeals C5-02-1766, 2003 (unpublished case).*

Substantial Compliance

The Court in <u>Larson v. Hendrickson,</u> *394 N.W.2d 524, 526 (Minn.App.1986),* held that rules governing service are liberally construed when the intended recipient had actual notice of the lawsuit, provided that is **substantial compliance** with Rule 4 of the Rules of Civil Procedure. *See* <u>Benny v. Pipes,</u> *799 F.2d 489, 492 (9th Cir.1986);* <u>Jackson v. Hayakawa,</u> *682 F.2d 1344, 1347 (9th Cir.1982).*

This **"Substantial compliance"** doctrine was also cited in an unpublished case titled <u>Central Internal Medicine Assoc. P.A.,vs. Keith V. Chilgren, et al.</u>, (unpublished 2000 Minn. Ct App C2-00-36) in which the Court held:

> *As this court recognized in **Times Square**, "A summons is 'a mere notice' that 'must substantially comply with the requirements of the rules' governing the service and form of process." **Id.** (quoting **Tharp v. Tharp**, 228 Minn. 23, 24, 36 N.W.2d 1, 2 (1949) and **Haas v. Brandvold**, 418 N.W.2d 511, 513 (Minn. App. 1988)) Similar to the challenge to the form of the summons in **Times Square**, the Chilgrens are objecting only to the form of the affidavit sent to the district court and not to the service of the summons itself. Because it is undisputed that the process server posted the summons and mailed a copy to the Chilgrens' last known address, "the function of the eviction notice was not negated by the minor technical error." **Id.** We conclude the district court had subject matter jurisdiction over this unlawful detainer action.*

When actual notice of the action has been received by the intended recipient, "the rules governing such service should be liberally construed." <u>Minnesota Mining and Manufacturing v. Kirkevold,</u> 87 F.R.D. 317, 323 (D.Minn.1980). <u>Larson v. Hendrickson,</u> 394 N.W.2d 524, 526 (Minn.App.1986). This "actual notice" exception, however, has been recognized only in cases involving substitute service at defendant's residence. See, e.g., <u>Minnesota Mining & Manufacturing Co. v. Kirkevold,</u> 87 F.R.D. 317 (D.Minn.1980). One reason for this approach is that there may be no place significantly more desirable for the papers to be left. <u>Wright & Miller, Federal Practice and Procedure,</u> § 1096 at 79 (2d ed. 1987). Rule 4 is otherwise taken literally, and cannot be satisfied by service on defendant's place of work or business. <u>Thompson v. Kerr,</u> 555 F.Supp. 1090, 1093 (D. Ohio 1982); Wright & Miller § 1096 at 74. Actual notice will not subject defendants to personal jurisdiction absent substantial compliance with Rule 4. See <u>Benny v. Pipes,</u> 799 F.2d 489, 492 (9th Cir.1986); Jackson v. Hayakawa, 682 F.2d 1344, 1347 (9th Cir.1982).

Minn. Stat. 504B.331 allows service by any person not named a party in the action. Issue is raised whether apartment manager or someone with Power of Authority can serve an eviction summons. Some Judges and Referees have applied "**de facto**" party rule. This rule states that if the person who serves the Summons and complaint has the "duties, responsibilities, rights and powers of the party named in the action", then this person is deemed to be a "de facto" party and may NOT service the Summons and Complaint.

Strict Compliance

In a recent 2013 Court of Appeals case, *Koski v. Johnson, A12-2274 (Minn. App. 2013)*, the Landlord attempt to evict Tenant and filed two affidavits with the court, the **Affidavit of Posting** and the **Affidavit of Not Found** verifying that two attempts to serve were made. Landlord failed to file the **Affidavit of Mailing** and **Affidavit of Plaintiff** as required by Minn. Stat. 504B.331. The District Court held that there was actual notice and therefore substantial compliance. This decision was reserved and the Court of Appeals held that strict compliance was required and all four affidavits must be filed. The Court of Appeals held as follows:

> We hold that section 504B.331 requires strict compliance, not merely substantial compliance. 2 To the extent that Times Square is contrary to that holding, we overrule it because it is unsupported by the cases on which we relied in Times Square and is contrary to Color–Ad Packaging, Inc. v. Kapak Indus., Inc., 285 Minn. 525, 526–27 & n.1, 172 N.W.2d 568, 569 & n.1 (1969), overruled on other grounds by In re Lake Valley Twp. Bd., Traverse Cnty. v. Lewis, 305 Minn. 488, 234 N.W.2d 815 (1975). In the cases on which we relied in Times Square, the summonses were governed by Minn. R. Civ. P. 4.01 and a district court rule, Haas, 418 N.W.2d at 513; Minn. R. Civ. P. 4.03, Pederson, 519 N.W.2d at 235; and Minn.Stat. § 543.02 (1948), Tharp, 228 Minn. at 24, 36 N.W.2d at 2, which "was superseded by [Minn. R. Civ. P.] 4.01," Shamrock Dev., 737 N.W.2d at 379 n.3. Notably, in Times Square, the partial quote from Pederson pertained to "a fundamental principle of the rules of civil procedure." 519 N.W.2d at 235 (emphasis added).

> "A party may waive a jurisdictional defense, including insufficient service of process, by submitting itself to the court's jurisdiction and affirmatively invoking the court's power." Shamrock Dev., 754 N.W.2d at 381. But Johnson did not do so here. Along with her answer, Johnson moved for dismissal or summary judgment, raising the issues of inadequate service and defenses on the merits. "Where a party simultaneously invokes the court's jurisdiction on the merits and asks the court to rule on a jurisdictional defense, waiver will not result unless other circumstances clearly demonstrate the party's acquiescence to the court's jurisdiction." Id. (quotation omitted). "[S]imple participation in the litigation does not, standing alone, amount to waiver of a jurisdictional defense. Rather, it is the failure to provide the court an opportunity to rule on the defense before affirmatively invoking the court's jurisdiction on the merits of the claim

that is determinative." Id. (quotation omitted). Although Johnson participated in the litigation, nothing in the record demonstrates her acquiescence to the court's jurisdiction.

53. Statute of Frauds-Leases

Minn. Stat. 513.05 provides that every contract for the leasing for a longer period than one year or for the sale of any lands, or any interest in lands, shall be void unless the contract, or some note or memorandum thereof, expressing the consideration, is in writing and subscribed by the party by whom the lease or sale is to be made, or by the party's lawful agent thereunto authorized in writing; and no such contract, when made by an agent, shall be entitled to record unless the authority of such agent be also recorded.

54. Stay of Eviction Action

Eviction proceedings are summary in nature. There are strict time guidelines required for eviction cases by statute. The Court has discretion to dismiss counterclaims related to title in eviction proceedings because of the summary nature of eviction actions.

The Court in ***Amresco Residential Mortgage Corp. vs. Stange***, 631 N.W. 2d 444, (Minn. App. 2001) held as follows:

> Defendants can raise their counterclaims and equitable defenses directly in a separate, district court proceeding, where they can also seek to enjoin prosecution of the eviction action. *William Weisman Holding Co. v. Miller*, 152 Minn. 330, 332, 188 N.W. 732, 733 (1922).

Amresco strikes a balance between the summary nature of eviction actions and Minn. Constitution Article 1, § 8. Fraser v. Fraser, 642 N.W.2d 34, 40 (Minn. App. 2002). While eviction cases are now heard by district courts with equitable powers, there is no need to interfere with the summary nature of eviction proceedings when there is an alternate process available for the resolution of challenges to the validity of a mortgage foreclosure underlying an eviction proceeding. Amresco, 631 N.W.2d at 446.

The Court of Appeals in ***Real Estate Equity Strategies, LLC v. Jones*** 720 N.W.2d 352 (Minn.App., 2006) stated as follows:

> The current limits on the scope of eviction proceedings are not based on an inability of the district court to adjudicate disputes other than the right to present possession of the premises. A tenant who challenges a landlord's title pursuant to Minn. Stat. § 504B.121 does not deprive the district court of subject-matter jurisdiction to hear the eviction proceeding.

Case-by-case determinations of whether to enjoin pursuit of eviction proceedings are both judicially more efficient (because the decision-maker may have more information and a broader spectrum of issues before it) and more consistent with **honoring the summary nature** of eviction proceedings. **We decline to adopt a universal requirement that eviction proceedings be stayed whenever a claim is asserted under chapter 325N.**

In summary, a Court may stay an eviction action if the parties have complicated issues regarding the property not because the court does not have jurisdiction, but more because eviction actions are summary proceedings, with limited rights of discovery, and trials must be scheduled within 6 business days. If there are legitimate title or other issues, it may be more appropriate for the case to be heard in a normal civil calendar rather than a summary court proceeding. Whether or not an eviction case should be stayed during the pendency of complicated litigation depends on the facts and the potential merits of Tenant's claims.

Stays under Minn. Stat. 325N are allowed in foreclosure reconveyance cases. See section above under "foreclosure reconveyance" for further discussion.

A common request for a stay in mortgage foreclosure cases is often made pursuant to <u>Bjorklund v. Bjorklund Trucking, Inc.</u> 753 N.W.3d 312 (Minn. App. 2008). The Court of Appeals in Bjorklund held that a district court abused its discretion by denying a motion to stay an eviction action when (1) an existing, separate district court action would be dispositive of the issues of possession and title to commercial real property involved in the eviction action and (2) the district court in the eviction action has concluded that some of the claims asserted in the first-filed action are essential to the defense of the eviction action.

The court in Bjorklund basically ruled that where the "counterclaims and defenses in the separate action are necessary to a fair determination of the eviction action, it is an abuse of discretion not to grant a stay of the eviction proceedings when an alternative civil action that involves those counterclaims and defenses is pending. Id at 318-19.

In a subsequent Court of Appeals case titled <u>Federal Home Loan Mortgage Corp. v. Nedashlovskly,</u> 801 N.W.2d 190 (Minn. Ct. App. 2011), the Court held that a party is **NOT entitled to a stay of an eviction action merely because a related action was filed first and is pending.** It held that the party seeking the stay must provide the court with a specific reason why a stay is appropriate or necessary to protect his/her interests.

It may be very difficult for the Judge or Referee assigned to the eviction case to determine whether a stay of the eviction case is appropriate or necessary. The District Court Judge assigned to the parallel or prior filed case will be in a better position to consider the Dahlberg or Dataphase factors and Rule 65 of the Minnesota or Federal Rules of Civil Procedure, which mandates the imposition of reasonable safeguards to protect the nonmoving party from harm. The District Court is also best suited to avoid inconsistent rulings when considering the moving party's likelihood of success on the merits of claims already before the district court and imposing reasonable bonding requirements, which again will protect the other party from frivolous claims and harm that would result from the injunction. See <u>Dahlberg v. Young</u> 42 N.W.2d 570 (Minn. 1950); <u>Dataphase Sys. Inc. v. CL Sys, Inc.</u> 640 F.2d 109, 113 8th Cir 1991).

In conclusion, Judges or Referees in eviction cases do have the discretion to stay eviction actions pursuant to the <u>Bjorklund</u> case under certain narrow circumstances provided they are able to articulate a specific reason why a stay is appropriate to protect the interests of the person in possession.

55. Tenancy at Sufferance

"Tenancy at will" means a tenancy in which the tenant holds possession by permission of the landlord but without a fixed ending date. In Minnesota, a tenant who wrongfully holds over after expiration of a lease without the consent of the Landlord becomes a **"tenant at sufferance."** *<u>Dvoracek v. Gillies</u>, 363 N.W.2d 99, 102 (Minn.App. 1985).*

The Minnesota Supreme Court held in <u>*Wiedemann v. Brown*</u> that a tenancy at sufferance occurs when the tenancy or estate or right has ended. The Court in <u>Wiedemann</u> added that a tenancy at sufferance "differs from the tenancy at will, where the possession is by the permission of the landlord." Therefore, if the person residing in the house has wrongfully held-over after the termination of his tenancy (i.e. if he was a tenant at will until the relative died and now he is holding-over wrongfully) then he would presumptively be a tenant at sufferance. <u>Wiedemann v. Brown</u> 250 N.W. 724, 727 (Minn. 1933).

The Restatement of Property provides a helpful summary regarding how a tenancy at will may be formed after the death of one of the parties:

> *The continuance of the tenancy at will depends upon the presence of the landlord's and tenant's wills that the tenancy continue. The death of either ends the presence of the will of the deceased, thereby bringing the tenancy to an end on the date the survivor becomes aware of the death, unless the decedent's successor in interest and the other party agree otherwise. If the landlord is the deceased, the successor to his interest by his actions may approve a new tenancy at will between him and the original tenant. Similarly, if the tenant dies, a new tenancy at will may be created by the agreement of the landlord and the person who succeeds to the deceased tenant's personal property. Restatement (Second) of Property, Landlord & Tenant §1.6 (1977).*

In Minnesota, the law does not require notice to terminate a tenancy at sufferance. In <u>*Dvoracek v. Gillies*</u> the Court found that Gillies had wrongfully held-over and became a tenant at sufferance because he had not properly sent notice to renew the lease as required by the lease. Id. The Court held that a letter that gave Gillies approximately two weeks to move out of the building had effectively terminated the tenancy at sufferance. In addition, Minn. Stat. Ann. §504B.135 does not apply to a tenancy at sufferance. This statutory section appears to create a three month notice requirement to terminate a tenancy at will where rent is not paid in cash such as this situation. However, by its terms this statute should only apply to a tenancy at will and not a tenancy at sufferance. Therefore, there is no statute in Minnesota which requires notice to terminate a tenancy at sufferance, and such a tenancy can be terminated upon the demand of the owner. In addition, if the tenant at sufferance refuses to quit the premises upon the demand of the owner, he could be liable to the landlord in an action for trespass.

56. Termination of Lease.

A lease may be terminated by express agreement or by implied agreement (sometimes called termination by operation of law), termination by estoppel, or acceptance of surrender. See Trimble v. Lake Superior & Puget Sound Co., 99 Minn. 11, 108 N.W. 867 (1906). A surrender by operation of law arises from a condition of fact that is voluntarily assumed and that is incompatible with the existence of a landlord-tenant relationship. Hildebrandt v. Newell , 199 Minn. 319, 323, 272 N.W. 257, 259 (1937). When, as here, the lease expressly permits re-entry by the landlord, there must be unequivocal proof that the landlord intended to forgive the tenant's further obligations under the lease and accepted the tenant's surrender of the premises. See Sjoberg v. Hartz, 199 Minn. 81, 84, 271 N.W. 329, 331 (1937). See also Provident Mutual Life Ins. Co. v. Tachtronic Instruments, Inc. 394 N.W.2d 161, Minn. App. 1986.

Minn. Stat. 504B.135 requires that a tenancy at will may be terminated by either party by giving notice in writing. The time of the notice must be at least as long as the interval between the time rent is due or three months, whichever is less.

Minn. Stat. 504B.135 also provides that if a tenant neglects or refuses to pay rent due on a tenancy at will, the landlord may terminate the tenancy by giving the tenant 14 days notice to quit in writing.

57. Title Defects or claims that Contract for Deed Cancellation or Mortgage Foreclosure procedure defective.

Eviction proceedings are summary in nature. There are strict time guidelines required for Eviction cases by statute. Court has discretion to dismiss counterclaims related to title in eviction proceedings because of the summary nature of eviction actions.

The Court in *Amresco Residential Mortgage Corp. vs. Stange*, 631 N.W. 2d 444, (Minn. App. 2001) held as follows:

> Defendants can raise their counterclaims and equitable defenses directly in a separate, district court proceeding, where they can also seek to enjoin prosecution of the eviction action. <u>William Weisman Holding Co. v. Miller</u>, 152 Minn. 330, 332, 188 N.W. 732, 733 (1922). Thus, there is no evident reason to interfere with the summary nature of eviction proceedings. Using the alternate procedure instead of expanding the eviction proceeding accords with the appellate courts' prior determinations that the district court should uphold the summary nature of eviction proceedings. *E.g.,* <u>Eagan East Ltd. P'ship v. Powers Investigations, Inc.</u>, 554 N.W.2d 621, 622 (Minn. App. 1996) (reversing decisions the court made on issues outside the limited scope of the proceeding). This process reinforces the public policy behind having summary proceedings, which is "to prevent parties from taking the law into their own hands." <u>Mutual Trust Life Ins. Co. v. Berg,</u> 187 Minn. 503, 505, 246 N.W. 9, 10 (1932). *See generally* Comment, *Landlord-Tenant Law: Abolition of Self-Help in Minnesota*, 63 Minn. L. Rev. 723 (1979).

The Court of Appeals in *Real Estate Equity Strategies, LLC v. Jones* 720 N.W.2d 352 (Minn.App., 2006) stated as follows:

> The current limits on the scope of eviction proceedings are not based on an inability of the district court to adjudicate disputes other than the right to present possession of the premises. A tenant who challenges a landlord's title pursuant to Minn. Stat. § 504B.121 does not deprive the district court of subject-matter jurisdiction to hear the eviction proceeding.
>
> Amici argue that allowing an eviction proceeding to finish before a chapter 325N action is resolved is inconsistent with chapter 325N because allowing the eviction proceeding to go forward allows the landlord, who may, in the chapter 325N action, be found to lack title to the property, to obtain possession of the property and possibly convey it. But amici's argument does not address the tenant's opportunities to (a) file a notice of lis pendens; (b) ask the chapter 325N district court to enjoin pursuit of the eviction proceeding; (c) recover compensatory damages in the chapter 325N action; (d) recover exemplary damages in the chapter 325N action, which, under Minn. Stat. § 325N.18, subd. 2 (2004), "shall not be less than 1-1/2 times the foreclosed homeowner's actual damages"; or (e) seek any other remedy available to the tenant as allowed by Minn. Stat. § 325N.18, subd. 3 (2004). Moreover, to the extent that the district court hearing a chapter 325N action has the information relevant to that action, that district court would be ideally situated to decide whether, to what extent, and under what conditions, to enjoin a related eviction proceeding. Case-by-case determinations of whether to enjoin pursuit of eviction proceedings are both judicially more efficient (because the decision-maker may have more information and a broader spectrum of issues before it) and more consistent with honoring the summary nature of eviction proceedings. **We decline to adopt a universal requirement that eviction proceedings be stayed whenever a claim is asserted under chapter 325N.**

58. Utilities

The most common basis for emergency tenant remedy actions is shut off of utilities. See Minn. Stat. 504B.215. If there is going to be a utility shutoff, this statute clarifies what information must be on shutoff notice given to Tenants and requires posting of shutoff notice to be in a conspicuous place.

If there is a utility shutoff, the Tenants have the right to have utilities restored if Tenant pays the **current charges for the most recent billing period.** Current charges does NOT include arrears or late payment fees incurred by Landlord. Minn. Stat. 504B.215 subd 3 now requires utility companies and municipalities to restore utility service if Tenant pays the current charges for the most recent billing period (limit of one time per 12 months period however). **This is a big change made in 2008 from prior law!**

This statute allows Tenant to deduct utility payments made from rent due. It also requires Tenant to provide documentation of payment made.

Single Meter Housing

In multiple unit housing (duplex or apartment buildings) a Landlord may not charge Tenants for pro-rated utility charges unless Tenants are provided information before they become a Tenant about the total utility cost for the building for each month of the most recent calendar year. Minn. Stat. § 504B.215, subd. 2a(1) requires notice to prospective tenants of the total utility cost for a single-metered residential apartment building for each month of the most recent calendar year when the landlord bills for utility charges separate from the rent. **Landlords cannot provide just an average, they must provide the actual monthly costs.** See Emerald Square Properties, Inc vs. Mackenzie Bailey Kutscheid 770 N.W.2d 529, Minn. App., August 11, 2009 (NO. A08-1620).

A collateral question then is raised if the court finds that Landlord breached Minn. Stat. 504B.215. What damages are Tenant entitled to if Landlord fails to provide Tenant with the actual monthly utility costs for the prior year?? The Court of Appeals in the Kutsheid case held that the damages provisions in Minn. Stat. 504B.221(a) does not apply to a violation of Minn. Stat. 504B.215, subd. 2a. (*Minn. Stat. 504B.221 provides for treble damages or $500.00 whichever is greater*). They did say however, that Tenant would be entitled to damages, if any, suffered because of Landlord failing to comply with Minn. Stat. 504B.215.

On Remand the District Court Referee ordered damages to Tenant in the amount of $1,798.67 which was the total amount of utilities paid by Tenant during the tenancy. The Referee found that since the Landlord violated the law regarding the utility payment this provision in the lease was unenforceable and there void.[25] This matter was then appealed to a District Court Judge who reduced the damages to $115.62.[26] The Judge determined the Tenant's damages by reimbursing the Tenant the difference between the highest billing amount represented by Landlord ($80) and the actual cost to Tenant over the course of the initial lease period ($89.83). This resulted in damages per month of $9.83. Both the Referee and the Judge awarded Tenant costs as allowed under Minn. Stat. 549.02 and attorneys fees of $500.00 as allowed by Minn. Stat. 504B.385 and 504B.425.

59. Venue

Minn. Statutes 542.02 states as follows: Actions for the recovery of real estate, the foreclosure of a mortgage or other lien thereon, the partition thereof, the determination in any form of an estate or interest therein, and for injuries to lands within this state, shall be tried in the county where such real estate or some part thereof is situated, subject to the power of the court to change the place of trial in the cases specified in section 542.11, clauses (1), (3), and (4). If the county designated in the complaint is not the proper county, the court therein shall have no jurisdiction of the action.

Minn. Stat. 542.11 allows the court to change venue in the following cases:

(1) upon written consent of the parties;

(2) when it is made to appear on motion that any party has been made a defendant for the purpose of preventing a change of venue under section 542.10;

(3) when an impartial trial cannot be had in the county wherein the action is pending; or

(4) when the convenience of witnesses and the ends of justice would be promoted by the change

60. Waiver

---

[25] The Court Referee provided the following legal support for his decision: 1) Any bargain that tends to a violation of the law is invalid and unenforceable. *Pettit Grain & Potato Co. v. Northern Pac. Ry. Co.*, 227 Minn. 225, 232-33, 35 N.W.2d 127, 131-32 (1948). 2) contracts against public policy are void. *Goodrich v. Northwestern Telephone Exchange Co.*, 161 Minn. 106, 110, 201 N.W. 290, 291-92 (1924); *Vercellini v. U.S.I. Realty Co.*, 158 Minn. 72, 73-74, 196 N.W. 672, 672 (1924); *Seitz v. Michael*, 148 Minn. 80, 85-86, 181 N.W. 102, 104 (1921). For purposes of a public policy analysis in association with a contract, legislative enactments are the public policy of the State of Minnesota. *Shank v. Fidelity Mut. Life Ins. Co.*, 221 Minn. 124, 130-31, 21 N.W.2d 235, 238 (1945). And 3) Illegal contractual provisions are stricken from a contract as unenforceable. *Dworsky v. Vermes Credit Jewelry, Inc.*, 244 Minn. 62, 65-66, 69 N.W.2d 118, 121-22 (1955).

[26] The Judge determined that where there is an illegality that occurs in some matter collateral to the contract, the contract is not thereby rendered illegal, unless the illegality taints the entire consideration of the contract. Ingersoll v. Randall 14 Minn. 400 (1869). The Judge then found that the Landlord's violation of Minn. Stat. 504B.215 was collateral to the lease and did not taint the entire consideration. The Judge then ordered the equitable remedy set forth above.

Waiver may be asserted as an affirmative defense in an unlawful detainer or (eviction) action. Priordale Mall Investors v. Farrington, 411 N.W. 2d 582 (Minn. App. 1987).

Landlords waive their right to evict Tenant if they accept a partial payment of rent in arrears and do not have an agreement that allows them to evict after accepting a partial payment. See Minn. Stat. 504B.291 (c).

Landlord may waive their right to evict a Tenant for breach of the lease if they accept a rent payment after the breach. In *Priordale Mall Investors v. Farrington* 411 N.W.2d 582 at 585 *(Minn. App. 1987)*, the Court held that Landlord waived it's right to evict the Tenant because Landlord accepted a rent payment after the alleged breach. The Court in Priordale held that waiver applied because a) the breach was only in the past and was not continuing. b) it accepted the rent from Tenant even though it knew of Tenant's breach, and c) it knew that one of Tenant's defenses to their eviction action was waiver.

If the breach is a continuing breach, and continues to exist after the acceptance of monthly rent, waiver may not apply. *Gluck v. Klkan, 36 Minn. 80, 81, 30 N.W. 446 (1886). Held that Landlord accepting rent from Defendant did not allow Defendant to continue the breach after paying the rent.* An example of a continuing breach would be having additional person residing in the leased property in violation of the lease.

For a recent unpublished Court of Appeals case that discusses the doctrine of Waiver, read Jack Christy vs. Douglas Berends, BES Auto Service, et al. Filed No. A07-1451 Filed July 22, 2008.

10. Judicial Review Checklist

The Judicial Review Checklist (Chapter 10) and the Emergency Review Checklist (Chapter 11) are for Judges who are asked to review a Referee's decision in the Fourth Judicial District.

Judicial Review Checklist

1. ☐ Determine who is present.

Judicial Reviews are generally heard on the Special Term Calendar. Pro Se parties can be represented by Agents in Housing Court Cases. Agents may represent artificial persons such as corporations and limited liability companies in Housing Court proceedings involving residential property. In the event of any appeal to District Court or the Court of Appeals, a licensed attorney must then represent a corporation as required by Minn. Stat. § 481.02. This is consistent with <u>Nicollet Restoration, Inc. vs. Turnham</u> 486 N.W. 2d 753 (Minn. 1992) which provided that a corporation must be represented by an attorney in an appeal from Conciliation Court to District Court for a trial de novo. The issue on whether or not agents can represent artificial persons in Housing Court involving commercial property is a bit more clouded, since they are not authorized to do so under Minn. Stat. §481.02 but appear to be authorized under Rule 603 of Housing Court. Because of this conflict, the Referees require that attorneys must represent artificial persons in Housing Court involving commercial properties.

2. ☐ Make sure you have copy of Transcript in File.

No new evidence should be received. *The review should be based only on the record established before the Referee. If you determine more evidence is needed you should either schedule a hearing to hear more evidence or remand back to the Referee with specific instructions. If no transcript has been provided by the party seeking review, the review must be dismissed unless the Referee has ordered that the transcript be waived. If there is no transcript even though it was timely ordered and any payment required for it timely made, Rule 611 allows the reviewing Judge to grant an extension of time to provide the transcript upon good cause shown.*

3. ☐ Ensure proper notice has been sent to opposing party.

4. ☐ Clarify legal issues to be reviewed. Legal issues should be clearly stated in Notice for Review.

5. ☐ Inquire about settlement possibilities.

Most Housing Court cases settle and sometimes after a few questions, you can remind the parties they are not far apart and if you have time, you may want to give them another chance to settle.

6. ☐ Hear Arguments and make decision

Judges need to affirm or reverse the Referee's order. It can be affirmed in part and reversed in part. If reversed, modify findings, conclusions and order accordingly. If the Referee erroneously excluded evidence that might have changed the outcome of the case, it can be used as part of the review decision. If you believe Referee made an error, it is very helpful to the Referee if you explain why you think he/she made a mistake.

7. ☐ <u>Do NOT expunge case</u> unless nothing further needs to be done on case.

Remember, if you expunge a case the file will be destroyed and nothing further can happen on the file. If you believe the file should be expunged, you either need to make sure the file is not expunged until everything you order can be completed, or in the alternative, you can simply allow the Tenant seeking expungement to make a motion to expunge and have the case heard on the Housing Court expungement Calendar which is scheduled once a month.

If Judges have any questions they may call either the Housing Court Referees or the Housing Court Supervisor at 612-348-2844 or 612-348-5186.

Other Notes

1. Reviews of Referee's Findings are governed by Minnesota Statute 484.70 and Rule 611 of the Housing Court Rules for Hennepin County.

2. Subdivision 7 Minnesota Statute 484.70 states as follows:

(a) All recommended orders and findings of a Referee shall be subject to confirmation by a Judge.

(b) Upon the conclusion of the hearing in each case, the Referee shall transmit to a Judge the court file together with recommended findings and orders in writing. The recommended findings and orders of a Referee become the findings and orders of the court when confirmed by a Judge. The order of the court shall be proof of such confirmation, and also of the fact that the matter was duly referred to the Referees.

(c) Review of any recommended order or finding of a Referee by a Judge may be by notice served and filed within ten days of effective notice of the recommended order or finding. The notice of review shall specify the grounds for review and the specific provisions of the recommended findings or orders disputed, and the court, upon receipt of a notice of review, shall set a time and place for a review hearing.

(d) All orders and findings recommended by a Referee become an effective order when countersigned by a Judge and remain effective during the pendency of a review, including a remand to the Referee, unless a Judge:

(1) expressly stays the effect of the order;

(2) changes the order during the pendency of the review; or

(3) changes or vacates the order upon completion of the review.

3. Rule 611 of the Housing Court Rules states as follows:

Rule 611. Review of Referee's Decision

(a) Notice. In all cases except conciliation court actions, a party not in default may seek judge review of a decision or sentence recommended by the Referee by serving and filing a notice of review on the form prescribed by the court administrator. The notice must be filed within ten days after an oral announcement in court by the Referee of the recommended order or within 13 days after service by mail of the adopted written order, whichever occurs first. Service of the written order shall be deemed complete and effective upon the mailing of a copy of the order to the last known address of the petitioner.

A judge's review of a decision recommended by the referee shall be based upon the record established before the Referee. Upon the request of any party, a hearing shall be scheduled before the reviewing judge.

(b) Stays. In civil cases, filing and service of a notice of review does not stay entry of judgment nor vacate a judgment if already entered unless the petitioner requests and the referee orders a bond, payment(s) in lieu of a bond, or waiver of bond and payment(s). The decision to set or waive a bond or payment(s) in lieu of bond shall be based upon Minn. R. Civ. App. P. 108, subdivisions 1 & 5. A hearing on a bond or payment(s) in lieu of bond shall be scheduled before the referee, and the referee's order shall remain in effect unless a judge modifies or vacates the order. In criminal cases, the execution of judgment or sentence shall be stayed pending review by the judge.

(c) Transcripts. The petitioner must obtain a transcript from the Referee's court reporter. The petitioner must make satisfactory arrangements for payment with the court reporter or arrange for payment in forma pauperis. Any transcript request by the petitioner must be made within one day of the date the notice of review is filed. The transcript must be provided within five business days after its purchase by the petitioner. For good cause the reviewing judge may extend any of the time periods described in this Rule 611(c).

4. Parties who were in default are NOT entitled to judicial review.

5. The non moving party is not required to appear or to file responsive papers but must be given notice of the review at least 10 days prior to the review date. The rules require that a hearing be set **upon the request of either party**.

6. The legal issues must be clearly stated in the Notice of Review.

7. No new evidence is to be received. The review is only on the record established before the Referee. (i.e. the transcript and the court file (pursuant to Rule 611 of the Housing Court Rules –Hennepin and Ramsey Counties). If no transcript has been provided by the party seeking review, the review must be dismissed unless the referee has ordered that the transcript be waived. If there is no transcript even though it was timely ordered and any payment required for it timely made, Rule 611 allows the reviewing Judge to grant an extension of time to provide the transcript upon good cause shown.

8. Judges need to affirm or reverse the referee's order. It can be affirmed in part and reversed in part. If reversed, modify findings, conclusions and order accordingly. If the referee erroneously excluded evidence that might have changed the outcome of the case, it can be used as part of the review decision.

9. If necessary, the case can be remanded back to the referee to further hearing.

10. If a Writ is stayed, either issue it, vacate it, or continue the stay for a specific time period on specific conditions.

11. Pursuant to Minn. Stat. 504B.345, Subd. 1, the Writ may be stayed up to 7 days if "immediate restitution of the premises would work a substantial hardship upon the defendant or defendant's family." In other words, if you are going to stay the Writ, you should have some sufficient reason to do so. You should NOT stay the writ if Tenant has been causing a nuisance or seriously endangering persons or property, or is being evicted for criminal activity on the premises. If the Writ is stayed pending a new trial, the issue of rent accruing in the interim may be addressed in the remand order if no bond has been posted. Issues regarding bond pending appeal should comply with the guidelines set out in Camber Hill Limited Partnership dba Camber Hill Townhomes vs. Edward Samuel, (Minn. Court of Appeals A06-6, 2006).

Standard of Review[27]

When reviewing a housing court referee's judgment, this court applies a clear error test. See In re Rudawski, 710 N.W.2d 264, 269 (Minn. 2006); Schuett Inv. v. Anderson, 386 N.W.2d 249, 252 (Minn. Ct. App. 1986). The Court will not determine that a finding is clearly erroneous absent a "clear demonstration that it is without substantial evidentiary

---

[27] The following information about Judicial Review of a Referee's decision is taken from a Memo prepared by Judge Gary Larson in the case Karmel Properties, LLC vs. Osman Mohamed d/b/a Qoraxlow Restaurant Court File No. 27-CV-HC-08-2708.

support or that it was induced by an erroneous view of the law." Schuett Inv., 386 N.W.2d at 252. Minnesota General Rules of Practice Rule 611(a) articulates this standard of review. Rule 611(a) states, "[a] judge's review of a decision recommended by the referee shall be based upon the record established before the referee." A hearing is not required. Id. Upon the request of any party, however, a hearing shall be scheduled before the reviewing judge. Id.

The issue of deference to the trial court, including a referee's, is addressed in Minn. R. Civ. P. Rule 52.01, which states in part, "[f]indings of fact, whether based on oral or documentary evidence, shall not be set aside unless clearly erroneous, and due regard shall be given to the opportunity of the trial court to judge the credibility of the witnesses." See also In re Rudawski, 710 N.W.2d at 269 (noting that when a referee makes findings of fact, those findings shall not be set aside unless clearly erroneous). Even when the reviewing court is ultimately responsible for the factual determination, the Minnesota Supreme Court has stated that the reviewing court must grant great deference to a referee's findings of facts. See Id. at 269 (noting that "this court gives . . . great deference to a referee's findings and will not reverse those findings unless they are clearly erroneous . . . .").

There is an issue whether a District Court Judge should review a Referee Order de novo. Minn. Gen. R. Prac. Rule 312 provides that review of a referee's findings or recommended order in family court "shall be based on the record before the referee and additional evidence shall not be considered, except for compelling circumstances constituting good cause." However, Minn. Gen. R. Prac. Rule 611 merely provides that review of a housing court referee's order "shall be based upon the record established before the referee." Rule 611 does not provide for circumstances when additional evidence shall be considered and, unlike Rule 312, restricts the district court's review of housing court matters to those "based upon the record established before the referee."

It is the long standing policy of Minnesota courts to defer in findings of fact to the court that actually heard the testimony. See Conroy v. Klienman Realty, 179 N.W.2d 162, 165-66 (Minn. 1970) (noting that the Court is "committed to the principle that the credibility of witnesses and the inferences fairly to be drawn therefrom are in the exclusive province of the trier of fact"). Those judicial officers have the opportunity to listen to the witnesses first hand, asses their demeanor, and determine credibility.

Although a transcript would assist a reviewing court to see whether the evidence meets the minimal levels required to sustain the court's findings, a transcript does not convey the qualitative aspects of testimony that the trial court observes. See In re Rudawski, 710 N.W.2d at 269 ("Although the referee's findings of fact are not binding in this case because Rudawski ordered a transcript, this court nonetheless gives great deference to a referee's findings and will not reverse those findings unless they are clearly erroneous . . .." (internal citations omitted)).

If Judges have any questions they may call Housing Court Referees Mark Labine (612-348-7731) or the Housing Court Supervisor at 612-348-7662 or 612-348-5186.

11. Emergency Review Checklist

Emergency Review Checklist

Parties will occasionally request a Judge do an Emergency review of a Referee Order.

Emergency reviews should be addressed only if a Judicial review is pending and should only address the issues set forth in Minn. Stat. 484.70 Subdivision 7(e). The most common request for emergency review will be to reduce the amount of bond ordered by the referee and in those cases the guidelines of the Camber Hill Limited Partnership should be followed. Another common request would be a review of the Referee's order denying Tenant's request to quash a Writ.

The inherent powers of emergency review as set forth in Subdivision 7(e) of Minn. Stat. 484.70 does not require notice to the opposing side or a hearing but judicial fairness would suggest that an opportunity for both sides to be heard on any issue before the Court would be proper.

1. ☐ Make sure that moving party has filed for a Judicial Review of an order under Rule 611 of the Housing Court Rules that is still pending.

2. ☐ Determine whether it is reasonable to try to notify other party to schedule a hearing.

Canon 2.9 of the Minnesota Code of Judicial Conduct provides that a Judge shall not initiate, permit or consider ex parte communications.... except as follows: 1) where circumstances require, ex parte communications for scheduling, administrative purposes, or emergencies that do not deal with substantive matters or issues on the merits...; provided: a) the judge reasonably believes that no party will gain a procedural or tactical advantage as a result of the ex parte communication and (b) **the judge makes provision promptly to notify all other parties of the substance of the ex part communication and allows an opportunity to respond.**

Canon 2.9 seems to say that you must make an effort to get the opposing side on the telephone or get them into court on short notice. If you can hear both sides of the issue, you are probably going to make a better decision.

3. ☐ Inquire whether moving party has already had an emergency review from another Judge.

Emergency Reviews should be assigned through Scheduling Office *and if this is done, this should not be an issue. Parties have been known to seek emergency reviews from more than one Judge, however, which should not be allowed.*

4. ☐ Address issue raised before you.

Usually the issue will be whether or not the supersedeas bond required to be posted pending the judicial review is too high or unreasonable. As stated in the cased Camber Hill Limited Partnership dba Camber Hill Townhomes vs. Edward Samuel, John Doe et. al., (Minn. Court of Appeals File No. A06-6) the "purpose of the supersedeas bond conditions is to assure that, pending the outcome of an appeal, the economic risk of the appeal is not borne by the party that prevailed below."

If Judges have any questions they may call Housing Court Referees Mark Labine (612-348-7731) or the Housing Court Supervisor at 612-348-7662 or 612-348-5186.

Other Notes

Emergency reviews are inherent in the power of Judges under Rule 60 of the Minnesota Rules of Civil Procedure to provide relief from a Judgment or Order and in Minn. Stat. 484.70 Subdivision 7(e) which allows the Judge to do as follows:

(e) All orders and findings recommended by a referee become an effective order when countersigned by a judge and remain effective during the pendency of a review, including a remand to the referee, unless a judge:

(1) expressly stays the effect of the order;

(2) changes the order during the pendency of the review; or

(3) changes or vacates the order upon completion of the review.

12. Administrators

The court may appoint an Administrator under Minn. Stat. 504B.425 if the court deems it necessary to resolve violations. The powers of the Administrator are described in section 504B.445. The court may direct that the administrator use the rents collected to remedy the violations found to exist by the court by paying the debt service, taxes, and insurance, and providing the services necessary to the ordinary operation and maintenance of the residential building which the landlord is obligated to provide but fails or refuses to provide.

After termination of administration, the court may continue the jurisdiction of the court over the residential building for a period of one year and order the landlord to maintain the residential building in compliance with all applicable state, county, and city health, safety, housing, building, fire prevention, and housing maintenance codes.

The administrator may be a person, local government unit or agency, other than a landlord of the building, the inspector, the complaining residential tenant, or a person living in the complaining residential tenant's dwelling unit. If a state or court agency is authorized by statute, ordinance, or regulation to provide persons or neighborhood organizations to act as administrators under this section, the court may appoint them to the extent they are available.

Powers of Administrator. The administrator may:

(1) collect rents from residential and commercial tenants, evict residential and commercial tenants for nonpayment of rent or other cause, enter into leases for vacant dwelling units, rent vacant commercial units with the consent of the landlord, and exercise other powers necessary and appropriate to carry out the purposes of sections 504B.381 and 504B.395 to 504B.471;

(2) contract for the reasonable cost of materials, labor, and services including utility services provided by a third party necessary to remedy the violation or violations found by the court to exist and for the rehabilitation of the property to maintain safe and habitable conditions over the useful life of the property, and disburse money for these purposes from funds available for the purpose;

(3) provide services to the residential tenants that the landlord is obligated to provide but refuses or fails to provide, and pay for them from funds available for the purpose;

(4) petition the court, after notice to the parties, for an order allowing the administrator to encumber the property to secure funds to the extent necessary to cover the costs described in clause (2), including reasonable fees for the administrator's services, and to pay for the costs from funds derived from the encumbrance; and

(5) petition the court, after notice to the parties, for an order allowing the administrator to receive funds made available for this purpose by the federal or state governing body or the municipality to the extent necessary to cover the costs described in clause (2) and pay for them from funds derived from this source.

The municipality shall recover disbursements under clause (5) by special assessment on the real estate affected, bearing interest at the rate determined by the municipality, but not to exceed the rate established for finance charges for open-end credit sales under section 334.16, subdivision 1, clause (b). The assessment, interest, and any penalties shall be collected as are special assessments made for other purposes under state statute or municipal charter.

Termination of administration. At any time during the administration, the administrator or any party may petition the court after notice to all parties for an order terminating the administration on the ground that the funds available to the administrator are insufficient to effect the prompt remedy of the violations. If the court finds that the petition is proved, the court shall terminate the administration and proceed to judgment under section 504B.425, paragraph (e).

Dwelling's economic viability. In considering whether to grant the administrator funds under subdivision 4, the court must consider factors relating to the long-term economic viability of the dwelling, including:

(1) the causes leading to the appointment of an administrator;

(2) the repairs necessary to bring the property into code compliance;

(3) the market value of the property; and

(4) whether present and future rents will be sufficient to cover the cost of repairs or rehabilitation.

504B.455 Removal of administrator.

Subdivision 1. Petition by administrator. The administrator may, after notice to all parties, petition the court to be relieved of duties, including in the petition the reasons for it. The court may, in its discretion, grant the petition and discharge the administrator upon approval of the accounts.

Subd. 2. Petition by a party. A party may, after notice to the administrator and all other parties, petition the court to remove the administrator. If the party shows good cause, the court shall order the administrator removed and direct the administrator to immediately deliver to the court an accounting of administration. The court may make any other order necessary and appropriate under the circumstances.

Subd. 3. Appointment of new administrator. If the administrator is removed, the court shall appoint a new administrator in accordance with section 504B.445, giving all parties an opportunity to be heard.

504B.461 Termination of administration.

Subdivision 1. Events of termination. The administration shall be terminated upon one of the following:

(1) certification is secured from the appropriate governmental agency that the violations found by the court to exist at the time of judgment have been remedied; or

(2) an order according to section 504B.445, subdivision 5.

Subd. 2. Accounting by administrator. After the occurrence of any of the conditions in subdivision 1, the administrator shall:

(1) submit to the court an accounting of receipts and disbursements of the administration together with copies of all bills, receipts, and other memoranda pertaining to the administration, and, where appropriate, a certification by an appropriate governmental agency that the violations found by the court to exist at the time of judgment have been remedied; and

(2) comply with any other order the court makes as a condition of discharge.

Subd. 3. Discharge of administrator. Upon approval by the court of the administrator's accounts and compliance by the administrator with any other order the court may make as a condition of discharge, the court shall discharge the administrator from any further responsibilities pursuant to section 504B.381 and sections 504B.395 to 504B.471.

State of Minnesota

<table>
<tr><td></td><td>**District Court**</td></tr>
<tr><td></td><td>Judicial District:
Court File Number:
Case Type: Housing</td></tr>
</table>

_____

Plaintiff

Order Appointing

Administrator

vs.

_____

Defendant

___

This case was heard by the undersigned on _____.

Date

PLAINTIFF: Represented by: ☐ counsel   ☐

agent

☐ Appeared in person.

☐ Did not appear and is in default.

_____   _____

Name

DEFENDANT: Represented by: ☐ advocate   ☐

counsel

☐ Appeared in person.

☐ Did not appear and is in default.   _____

Name

        Based upon the verified petition, testimony, evidence, and arguments presented, and all of the files, records, and proceedings, the Court makes the following:

Findings Of Fact

1. This matter involves residential premises located at _____.

2. Rent for the property is $_____.00 per month. Other rent provisions are as follows:

_____.

3. The premises were found to be in violation of Minn. Stat. 504B.161 as follows:

4. In a prior court order, Defendant was ordered to provide evidence of a rental license and to complete all repairs required to correct the code violations at the property. Defendant has failed to do so.

5. The Tenant petitioned the court to appoint _____. as Administrator with powers under Minn. Stat. 504B.445 Subd. 5.

6. The Landlord has failed to comply with the prior court's orders to repair the code violations. The Court finds that the appointment of an Administrator is appropriate in this case to ensure that the code violations are corrected.

7. _____. is willing to be appointed Administrator of the leased property. The estimated costs of the repairs needed to bring the leased property up to code is approximately $_____, including the administrator fee.

8. Current monthly rent for the leased property of $_____ makes it economically viable to appoint the Administrator pursuant to Minn. Stat. 504B.445 subd. 8.

9. The fair market value of the leased property according to the property tax statement is $_____.

Conclusions Of Law

1. The leased property is economically viable to appoint the Administrator pursuant to Minn. Stat. 504B.445 subd. 8.

2. Minn. Stat. 504B.425 allows the Court to appoint an Administrator if Landlord fails to remedy code violations at leased property after being ordered to do so. The Administrator's powers and duties are set out in Minn. Stat. 504B.445.

Order

1. _____ **is appointed Administrator** of the property located at _____.

2. That the Administrator shall comply with the ordinances of the City of _____ and shall acquire a rental license for the property in the Defendant's name;

3. That the Administrator is not required to post a bond in this matter;

4. Tenant shall pay her portion of rent directly to the Administrator commencing with the next months rent.

5. The Administrator must first contract and pay for residential building repairs and services necessary to keep the residential building habitable before other expenses may be paid. Second, the Administrator should pay any association fees owed for the leased property since the Association uses these fees to care for the property. If sufficient funds are available, the Administrator shall pay other expenses, such as tax and mortgage payments. If sufficient funds are not available for paying other expenses, such as tax and mortgage payments, after paying for necessary repairs and services, the landlord is responsible for the other expenses as provided by Minn. Stat. §504B.445 Subd. 4.

6. That after the Administrator completes the repairs, they shall make an accounting to
the court with the motion to discharge the Administrator. The motion to discharge shall be heard at a compliance hearing before this court. At that hearing the Administrator will present an accounting of work done and will request reasonable fees for service as the Administrator. At that hearing the court will also hear arguments for the award of rent abatement to Plaintiff and reasonable attorney's fees to Plaintiff's counsel.

7. **Administrator Expenses**. The court shall allow a reasonable amount for the services of administrators and the expense of the administration from rent money. When the administration terminates, the court may enter judgment against the landlord in a reasonable amount for any unpaid services and expenses incurred by the administrator.

8. **Powers**. Under Minn. Stat. 504B.445, The administrator may:

(a) collect rents from residential and commercial tenants, evict residential and commercial tenants for nonpayment of rent or other cause, enter into leases for vacant dwelling units, rent vacant commercial units with the consent of the landlord, and exercise other powers necessary and appropriate to carry out the purposes of sections 504B.381 and 504B.395 to 504B.471;

(b) contract for the reasonable cost of materials, labor, and services including utility services provided by a third party necessary to remedy the violation or violations found by the court to exist and for the rehabilitation of the property to maintain safe and habitable conditions over the useful life of the property, and disburse money for these purposes from funds available for the purpose;

(c) provide services to the residential tenants that the landlord is obligated to provide but refuses or fails to provide, and pay for them from funds available for the purpose;

(d) petition the court, after notice to the parties, for an order allowing the administrator to encumber the property to secure funds to the extent necessary to cover the costs described in clause (2), including reasonable fees for the administrator's services, and to pay for the costs from funds derived from the encumbrance; and

(e) petition the court, after notice to the parties, for an order allowing the administrator to receive funds made available for this purpose by the federal or state governing body or the municipality to the extent necessary to cover the costs described in clause (2) and pay for them from funds derived from this source.

9.   **Special Assessment.** The municipality may recover disbursements under paragraph 3e above by special assessment on the real estate affected, bearing interest at the rate determined by the municipality, but not to exceed the rate established for finance charges for open-end credit sales under section 334.16, subdivision 1, clause (b). The assessment, interest, and any penalties shall be collected as are special assessments made for other purposes under state statute or municipal charter.

10. **Termination of administration.** At any time during the administration, the administrator or any party may petition the court after notice to all parties for an order terminating the administration.

11. **Administrator's liability.** The administrator may not be held personally liable in the performance of duties under this section except for misfeasance, malfeasance, or nonfeasance of office.

12. The Clerk of Court shall either give to the parties or mail to the parties by first class mail a copy of this Order.

Let Judgment Be Entered Accordingly

By the Court

_____ _____
Judge   Date

Judgment

I hereby certify that the above Order constitutes the entry of Judgment of the Court.

Dated: _____   Court Administrator
                                                                          By:
                                                                                    Deputy

13. Index

Made in the USA
San Bernardino, CA
07 March 2016